the Heart of Spain

FAMILIES AND FOOD

DONALD B. HARRIS

Duende Press . Williamsburg, Virginia

Published by Duende Press
www. HeartOfSpainBook.com

Jacket design by Dunn+Associates, www.dunn-design.com
Interior design by Dorie McClelland, Spring Book Design
Cover photographs: Happy pigs - Sánchez Romero Carvajál; All other photographs –
Harris family

Printed in Canada

Library of Congress Cataloging-in-Publication Data
Harris, Donald B.
        The Heart of Spain: Families and Food
ISBN: 978-0-9827721-0-2 (hardcover)
Spain—Description and Travel
Spain—Social Life and Customs
Spain—Food

Other books by Donald B. Harris:
That's How the Light Gets In: A Credo of Friendship, 1994, Credo Institute
To purchase, email credooffriendship@gmail.com
Describes a pioneering Navy program the author founded in the 1970's to help alienated
personnel, many with post-traumatic stress. Through the powerful vehicle of music the
CREDO Weekend helped people to articulate their inner struggles and find acceptance
within the caring community that formed among the gathered participants. Variations of
the program are still ongoing in the USN and USMC, and in the civilian world.

For

My dear wife Ruth,
beloved helpmate and companion,
without whom I do not feel complete

My family: sons, wives and grandchildren,
whose constant love brings such joy

My brothers and sisters of Spain,
who continue to enrich our lives

CONTENTS

❦

Food, Culture and Friends

6 Fiestas and Celebrations

7 Closing Thoughts

*Spanish translations of the original essays may be found
on the author's blog at www.latienda.com or blog.tienda.com.*

Happy churro eater—Jim Fernandez

An Unusual Feast

This collection is an unusual feast for the reader. Most books about food feature celebrity cooks on the one hand, confiding to us the marvels and magic of their culinary skills, or populist cooks on the other, encouraging us in the possibility of achieving our own down-home French or frugal or low cal cuisine. Don Harris, a Merchant Prince of a man really, is up to something quite different. He wants us to know something about the people, the families mostly, who produce the Spanish artisan foodstuffs he and his family offer to Americans and Europeans in their Virginia store and on line through *La Tienda.com*. And, indeed, we come to know in these pages the many individuals and families throughout Spain whose careful artisan cultivation and elaboration is responsible for the foodstuffs that Harris purveys. One has to say "throughout Spain." Is there anyone who has visited more widely in Spain over the last forty some years and who has come to know and make friends with as many people throughout the peninsula as have he and his wife?

But we get to know more here than about food, people and places. Don Harris also wants us to know some essential things about the Spanish culture in which these foodstuffs are produced. He feels, and wants us to also feel and ponder the particular "charm" (*duende*) of Spain. Its "heart" or "soul" as he calls it. Thus he keeps a steady eye trained on its history and culture. He provides an instructive "time binding" to the past in many of his vignettes. We learn much about local and national history. We learn, for example, about how central the Spanish role has been in the history of chocolate. We discover her important role in bringing foodstuffs—rice, saffron, almond pastes etc.—to the west from the ancient Middle East through the long presence in the Iberian Peninsula of the Moors and of Islam. We learn much, indeed, about the debt Spanish food culture owes to the Moors. We learn about the history of the cultivation of the haba bean, about saffron, about the exquisite ibérico hams produced in the acorn forests of the south and west, about the shellfish fisheries and quality canneries of Galicia and the Levante. We see how the pressing of olive oil has changed since early Roman times, and how some are preserving old methods. We discover how the fortified wines of southern Spain—the sherries of Don's "home away from home," El Puerto de Santa María, Cádiz—captured the English nose and palate.

The author's pursuit of the "heart and soul" of Spain is therefore thematic throughout the collection. He finds it, mainly, in the continuities and stabilities of family life extended in time and confined in space, and in Spaniards' careful attention to the well-being of the next generation—their love for children. These values contrast significantly with the "personal autonomies" and constant itinerancy and separation that characterize much of the life of American families. Though one of the author's sections of the collection is entitled *Zarzuela* (*Pot Pourri*), a section treating such topics as the El Camino pilgrimage and bull fighting, there is everywhere in the collection this guiding thematic search and energizing and organizing interest.

I think it admissible to refer, perhaps hyperbolically, to Don Harris as a "Merchant Prince of a man" because, after all, he is a merchant. But he is a merchant of a certain generosity, even nobility, of character vis a vis his fellows and especially those artisans who plant, weed, harvest, herd and, husband, press, bake, confect and bottle or can, in short, those who pick, produce and prepare the wines, olive oils, hams, chorizos, cheeses, sweets and other baked goods he and his family make available on this side of the Atlantic or in the north of Europe. Those of us of direct descent or indirect inheritance from the Peninsula can only be grateful for what La Tienda makes available to us, feeding so well our gustatory nostalgia in our displacement in the New World.

But this collection is not just for those who treasure an Iberian ancestry and are nostalgic for its foods in their New World displacement. It is also for those, many of whom are strangers to Spain, who are seeking to come to know Spain better; its foods, of course, but also something of its long enduring history and culture—the ultimate context of these many foodstuffs.

For some half dozen years before and after my retirement I spent the month of January in Barcelona, teaching an intensive "Antiquity and Modernity" course for the Mediterranean Civilization Foreign Study Sequence of the University of Chicago. In orienting new students, so they might more readily learn from their upcoming experience before flying overseas, I regularly recommended that they access Don Harris's essays on the Internet at *LaTienda.com*. His vignettes would give them, I told the students, an instructive and sympathetic introductory look into the country in which they would be studying. Moreover, as most of these vignettes are anchored in the countryside, amidst the family producers of "the bread of Spanish life" so to speak, they would become more grounded in Spanish life than they otherwise might ever be, living as they would be the purely urban existence of their Barcelona term abroad.

To be sure I think that Spaniards, *Celt-Iberians* as they call themselves, or those descended from them like myself, will occasionally feel that Don Harris is generous to a fault in appraising the qualities of Spanish character. Most Spaniards are too aware of their many defects that their history has shown over and over again. But still it is a fine and gratifying thing to see also our virtues, our fundamental hospitality and congeniality, our sense of responsibility towards our traditions and the qualities of the family life we treasure and the artisan products we produce, so generously recognized. It is not all that frequent an assessment in North European or North American lands where old Imperial, north-south, conflicts with the Mediterranean World and the negative stereotypes these conflicts have produced are still present, if only in a sublimated form.

Don Harris's authority is supported by extraordinary experience. To repeat the point in a different way, I doubt that there is another American or North European who has had over these forty years—since Harris's early years a s a Navy chaplain in the American base in Rota, Cádiz—as wide an experience of the many parts and many foods of Spain. It's a blessing, frankly, to have Don Don, his wife Ruth and their extended family inscribe here their long experience, for us to savor in so many different ways in so many different Spanish places in so many different vignettes.

So read on lucky reader. Don't eat it all at one sitting, though if you do you will get a view, of rare appreciative detail, into the unity and variety of a nation. Sample the various vignettes a few at a time. Begin, if you like, with one of my two favorites: in Section 3, for example," Medina Sidonia-Sweet Irony." This is a story, lodged in history, of the Moorish and Islamic sweets that have come to be the center of the Spanish Christmas. Or begin with "Nochebuena in the Alpujarras" in Section 6. This is a Christmas adventure of the Harris family in the mountains of southeastern Spain in which local hospitality triumphed over a formidable winter storm. The preceding or succeeding riches of this Harris collection should give you many days of pre- or post-prandial pleasure, I feel quite sure. It has surely done so for this writer, his wife and students. This book is sure to provide you with reiterated interest in Spain, its people and the various staffs of life that nourish it. And it may even provide you with a sense of kinship with those who produce the Spanish foods you will be eating and with those, the Harris family, who make them available to us here at home!

James W. Fernandez
Professor Emeritus of Anthropology
University of Chicago

❦

The Don, the Pioneer

I met Don Harris in the fall of 2009. It was during the Society of Spain's Admiral Menendez Awards Gala in Washington, D.C. That night, Mr. Harris received the Admiral Menendez Friend of Spain Award, the General Consul of El Salvador Ana Margarita Chávez was honored with the Amigo de España Award, and I was distinguished with the Admiral Menendez Pioneer Award. At the end of the dinner, I went to the table where Don and his wife Ruth were still talking to Chef José Andrés, who had introduced Don to an audience of Spaniards and Americans with words of respect, admiration, and "cariño."

I said to him, "Sir, you are a true pioneer and my reward tonight would be having the privilege of your friendship." I remember engaging in a conversation around my three favorite "fs": Food, Family and Fun. With fervor, we talked about our children, and how Spanish roots enrich our Americaness. We passionately agreed that there is nothing more fulfilling and meaningful than connecting the cultural and spiritual dots across the Atlantic.

A year later, that conversation continues.

I first heard of Don in the late 1990s, when I was a lecturer of Spanish language and literature at Johns Hopkins University in Baltimore. I got to know him through his company, LaTienda.com, which became my favorite online spot for academic projects with which to inflict joyful torture upon my students. Even my wife, Zuni, used the site for some of her high school classes. The idea of an online store was a great deal in the early years of the www boom. But this was a store specialized in the food and

Don Harris receives the 2009 Friends of Spain Award, along with Ana Margarita Chávez, Consul General of El Salvador and Alberto Avendaño, El Tiempo Latino

the cultural flavors of Spain. It was the idea of a gringo who not only had a business model in his hands but the passion to put together a project closer to his heart than to his wallet.

Don's love for Spain transcends a successful business—a family business. He found in my original land, in my landscapes, in my territories . . . food to feed the soul and peoples to vindicate the essence of humanity. What Don has done with our beloved Iberia is dig into its essence. Don Harris has the eye of an explorer, the taste of a gourmet, the touch of a painter, and the sense of a spiritual teacher.

He writes about flavors, family, and feelings with generosity and simplicity. And the reader feels that a gift is being given. The main characters of Don's narrative are Don Ignacio, Lola, José, Amalia, Pepe, Jorge . . . artisans, Maestros of food and flavors, human beings with Iberian pride and rich roots.

In his first book, *That's How the Light Gets In*, Don Harris gives us the key to understanding his approach to Spain as soul matter: "When we are able to suspend the objective—the 'shoulds' and 'musts', the correct and the incorrect—then we are able to comprehend the totality of what we seek to understand. We are able to see its *charisma*: its spiritual essence."

The Admiral Menendez Awards Gala of 2009 took place in La Taberna del Alabardero, a Spanish culinary enclave in the nation's capital. We enjoyed a tapas cocktail of baby octopus, potato and paprika brochette, manchego cheese brochette with sherry tomato, salmon tartar with vegetables, codfish and parsley croquettes, and piquillo peppers stuffed with braised ox tail. This started the dialogue. We continued with cauliflower cream and "de la vera" paprika oil emulsion, Tolosa asparagus stuffed with Basque-style crab meat, sautéed spinach and lobster bisque, and hake in garlic-parsley sauce with clams and asparagus. And wines: Albariño, Rioja and Cava. This prepared us for the awards.

I was honored that night to share the stage with Don Harris, because he greatly deserves what was written on the award: "For Outstanding Leadership and Dedication on Behalf of Spain and Spanish Culture."

> Alberto Avendaño is an award winning writer, journalist, and translator who has divided his life and career between Spain and the United States. He is also Director of Business Development for *El Tiempo Latino,* the Spanish language publication of *The Washington Post*.

The Harris family

For Love of Spain

I would like to share with you a compilation of reflections that I have been writing since 1997. From the beginning the essays have focused on the way of life of people I met in Spain, and the values they encouraged within me as a young father. I initially wrote these reflections for friends I made through La Tienda, the online retail company my family and I began in the early days of the Internet. I wanted to encourage an appreciation of the values and integrity of this ancient culture as they are realized today in the lives of the Spanish families who prepare the food we import for our tables.

Often I have been asked, "How is it that the Harris family, without a drop of Spanish blood, (that we know of), ends up being a leading source of fine Spanish food in America?"

It all goes back to our family; the ties we feel toward each other and how they mirror the best of the Spanish family tradition. We were a Navy family, with all this entails. Ninety days after Ruth and I were married, I was ordered to serve as chaplain for a Mediterranean-bound destroyer squadron. Ruth was left among a pile of moving boxes in Norfolk. Yet it turned out to be a blessing, as my Spanish port calls changed our lives. There, for the first time, I experienced traditional Spanish culture where family ties are strong and children are cherished.

For some families the sailor's life is too unpredictable and creates strains. For other families, such as ours, the unpredictability and uncertainty of Navy life encourage closeness and bonding that might not be necessary in a more settled circumstance. It is a hard life, but one full of adventure. We moved twenty-six times. Tim, our eldest was born in Virginia; Jonathan in San Diego. Christopher is our Spanish son. He even has a birth certificate from Rota in Cádiz, emblazoned with "Hijo de la Raza"!

Our kids had to fit in with classmates of many schools. Tim set the record with thirteen different schools before college. Jonathan was in three fourth grades! They did not have the luxury of taking many years to build friendships, so of necessity formed them within their family. I remember many times Ruth and I would urge the boys to make friends in the new neighborhood. They invariably replied, "Why? We have our brothers."

When the Navy gave us our dream assignment in Spain, Ruth and I saw in the typical Andaluz family the same kind of closeness and interdependence that we fostered as parents. Our family grew strong because constant change made close relationships within the family vital. Paradoxically, the Spanish family forms lasting bonds because there is no change at all. They have years—even generations—to build family ties.

Whether in Spain or America, it takes hard work and commitment to foster healthy family relationships. People are people anywhere on the globe; we are all imperfect, to be sure. But with the model of a loving extended family as the ideal, it is easier to keep your eye set on the goal.

Spanish families are quite communal and regularly share meals together. They also have a strong sense of hospitality for the stranger, who is treated as a friend. When we visited a Spanish family we could count on sharing tapas or a freshly prepared meal with them, either at home or at their favorite local restaurant.

When we were stationed in Spain, we elected to live with the Spanish people, rather than on the base. We wanted to be immersed in their generous life, to experience firsthand the culture we found so appealing. Ruth and I rented a traditional home among the sherry bodegas in the oldest section of El Puerto de Santa María, a nearby town. Tim was five years old and Jonathan was only two. The house was located along the main street, Calle Larga, around the corner from a Moorish castle. The air was laden with the heady aroma of aging wine, and often we heard young people clapping flamenco rhythms as they walked down the cobblestone street. Later we moved to a chalet in a more secluded area where our youngest son Christopher was born.

We enrolled Tim in El Centro Inglés where he spent the school day with Spanish kids as well as a few English and Americans.

Tim valued his experience at the school so much that he and Amy spent the first six months of 2010 in the same neighborhood where he grew up, and sent their two boys, Ben and Sam, to a small school in Jerez de la Frontera. There, they spent every school day with a mix of children from Spanish and English-speaking families, just as Tim experienced before.

When we were in Spain, at a moment's notice we would pile the kids into the car (no cumbersome car seats in those days) and head north, showing them castles, Romanesque and Visigothic churches, and beautiful old town such as Trujillo, Guadalupe, Cáceres, Úbeda, Jaén, Cuenca, and Soria. I must admit that sometimes their eyes glazed over as we showed them yet another church, but castles were no problem.

Santiago de Compostela always struck a chord with our family—so much so that many years later when Jonathan was a young man in college he spent one summer walking across the north of Spain to Santiago on the pilgrimage route, Camino de Santiago. Later, he and his bride Stacey walked from León to Santiago on their honeymoon. Our youngest son, Chris, spent a summer in La Coruña as a college student, and Tim spent a summer with Spanish friends in Sevilla.

We grew to be a close, cohesive family with a shared love for Spain, whose culture was built on the same foundation of family as ours. Later, when we were stationed in the United States we would take the boys back to Spain, revisiting our old haunts and finding new people and places to enjoy. On the return flight we would load an extra suitcase with memories of Spain: those long tube glasses they use at tapas bars, ceramics and cazuelas of all sorts, María cookies and, most of all, bars of Heno de Pravia and Magno soaps whose familiar fragrance still waft through our home.

When I retired from the Navy, we settled in Williamsburg, Virginia where I had attended college. Ruth and I decided to dress up our house with lots of classic Moorish-style tile to remind us of our happy years in Andalucía. We adorned our bathrooms, kitchen, fireplace and dining room with classic Moorish designs reminiscent of the Alhambra.

When our two older sons began making lives of their own after college, a serious medical situation occurred at home, which caused the family to draw even closer. As the medical crisis was resolved, we realized how much we enjoyed each other's company and thought of ways we could work together in a common enterprise.

It was the early days of the Internet. While Tim worked with a Virginia ham company, Jonathan, with a degree in fine arts, experimented with web design. Since Spanish tiles were hard to find and we had found good sources, Jonathan posted them on the web to help others with their quest for authentic tiles. With that action, La Tienda was born, just a year after Amazon.com started.

Soon Tim suggested adding a picture of a jamón serrano to our tile site, to see whether anyone would like one if we could import it. The response was immediate and enthusiastic, and I began writing our customers monthly about our progress toward bringing Spanish ham to their American table. It was clear that La Tienda had made contact with the Spanish soul.

Today La Tienda has grown into far more than Ruth and I had ever dreamed, and our family continues to work in concert. Our sons Tim and Jonathan share the same office with me. Their wives Amy and Stacey are an integral part, and contribute on a regular basis while looking after their four little children. Our youngest son Chris never got the wandering lust out of his bones. He and his wife, Rian, travel the globe as diplomats for the U.S. State Department, and keep close contact with the progress of the family company through the Internet and Skype. The whole family continues to travel the byways of Spain. We enjoy meeting families with small artisan businesses and selecting their products for La Tienda. We find great satisfaction in supporting their families and a way of life with which we resonate.

In our veins flow the blood of the Dutch, Frisians, Scots-Irish, English and Armenians—we are American, from immigrant stock. But our hearts have absorbed the essence of Spain and we feel at home there. After all, our wanderings across the landscape of Spain reach back to 1965! We find it a source of joy to work together, and to bring others our love for traditional Spain, as expressed in their cuisine and through my reflections in this book.

The Engaging People of Spain

A few years ago, I offered an older lady my favorite bonbon—a fig stuffed with dark chocolate and brandy. She waved her finger and said warmly, "No thank you, I don't eat figs anymore." She explained, "When I was a little girl in Zaragoza, figs were the only food we had to eat. The Civil War was a terrible time, and World War II was worse."

As we talked further among the group of shoppers getting their last minute polvorones, mantecados and jamón at our Christmas shop, (and with the encouragement of family members) she burst out singing a "jota"—melancholy blues from traditional Aragón. Her strong, clear voice sang of the River Ebro and the struggles of her people. Then with a twinkle in her eye and a warm embrace, she gathered her turrón, jamón and other treats, and said, "I must go now. Feliz Navidad."

That lady from Zaragoza, who has lived a life of suffering and joy, captured for me that indefinable quality which is Spain: a personal engagement and joyful resilience with a hint of melancholy that I have experienced in no other country.

I met my first Spaniard almost forty-five years ago at about two in the morning. He was a young bartender at Casa Ángel, a tiny café in Valencia, and I was a young naval officer who had just walked off the gangway of my destroyer to explore the Gothic Quarter of town late at night. I dropped into a small tapas bar that was nearly deserted except for a trio of gypsies quietly singing in the corner with their guitars. The young man welcomed me as if

Cheerful ladies display local cheeses, Central Market, Lugo (Lugo)

I were an old friend, and while we were awkwardly talking to each other in two languages, he prepared a cazuela of gambas al ajillo, garlic shrimp sizzling in olive oil. When I told him how much I enjoyed it, he wrote out his special recipe and gave it to me saying, "Try this recipe when you get home. Maybe you could name it "Gambas Ángel."

Since that time, I have found that this kind of spontaneous generosity is a distinguishing characteristic of the Spanish culture. Hospitality is extended to all: whether you are a visitor or one of their extended family. It seems second nature for the Spaniard to want to spend time with you around a table spread with freshly prepared food. The Spaniard knows instinctively that eating together is central to our identity as humans.

The following spring I brought over my bride Ruth to share in the magic. In due course we passed on our appreciation of the Spanish people to our three boys—especially during the time we all lived in Andalucía. Sometimes

Legendary churro maker Charo Salguero Venega and son, Mercado Municipal,
El Puerto de Santa María (Cádiz)

when you are welcomed into a different culture you appreciate it more than if
you are born into it.

We lived among generous people in the sherry town of El Puerto de Santa
María. Our Spanish neighbors offered their hospitality, even though we were
strangers. We were most impressed when we saw how their extended families
were the foundation of their lives. Their children were precious, and were
embraced within the family as well as the neighborhood within which they
would be nurtured.

Many years ago, when my eldest son Tim was a student at El Centro Inglés,
a bilingual preschool, he and his little classmates returned home in the middle
of every school day. It was natural to include in the schedule a three-hour
siesta so that the young children could relax at lunch with their families. It
was not the hurried lunch in the school cafeteria that Tim's sons now experience in Virginia!

The routines of traditional Spain accommodate life's natural rhythms. They affirm what is important for a spiritually healthy life: the centrality of the family, the need for respite in the middle of the workday, and the need for broader community. After the workday concludes in smaller towns, many people plan to drop by the same café that they have for years. They love to talk with their friends—many of whom they have known since they were children together!

This rhythm leads to an intrinsic stability, punctuated by many fiestas, ferias and saints' days. Every occasion, even shopping at the market, or lingering at a cafe is treated as an event—an opportunity to be with friends and neighbors.

Recently Tim and I dropped by a shore-side restaurant in Sanlúcar de Barrameda, where we were looking forward to a lunch of little clams called coquinas, and some of the famous Sanlúcar langostinos. When we saw how expensive the seafood was it caused us to have second thoughts, but that did not faze the young working-class family at the next table. They were having a great time laughing together as they feasted on a large platter of the freshest shellfish. At first I was quite surprised at the money they were spending, but then it occurred to me that they had their priorities right. A feast with loved ones is also food for the soul.

When visiting those in Spain who provide products for La Tienda, I can hardly recall a time that we did not seamlessly migrate to the dinner table. There we could forge bonds that transcended business, enjoying each other's company and the conversation about our families and the delicious meal before us.

I think we all know that when we set aside a regular time to eat together with our children, looking at their faces and hearing their stories, having a meal becomes not just a way to assuage our hunger but an occasion to build bonds of caring and love. We miss something important when we choose to skip meals altogether or graze at convenience stores where our only contact with others is waiting in line with our paper cups of coffee.

I read an excellent article "Out of the Kitchen, Onto the Couch" in the August 2, 2009, issue of the *New York Times Magazine* that suggested that eating a meal together might even go to the heart of our identity as human beings. When taken seriously as a human activity, sharing a meal that we have prepared is very important to our happiness and to our health.

According to the author, Michael Pollan, cooking makes us who we are. It is a symbolic way of distinguishing ourselves from the animals. He says that cooking is a metaphor for the human transformation of nature into culture; anthropologists have begun to take quite literally the idea that cooking is the key to our humanity. For our early ancestors, it was the discovery of fire and then cooking and eating together—not just tool making or language—that made us human. Paleolithic art in the Altamira caves reveals our earliest ancestors depicting their hunt for game.

If we let ourselves be governed by the Food Police we miss the sacredness of the occasion. How many a dinner is drained of joy by discussions of calories and fiber, or the mercury content of the beautifully prepared fish before us! Breaking bread together gives us not just physical nourishment but also the occasion of being together at an appointed time and place, and sharing something deeper.

As the years unfold, new factors and the accompanying attitudes that emerge compete with the underlying structure of traditional society. As Spain arises from its slumber and trades with Europe and the world, urban values crowd out the traditional: a siesta becomes "inefficient" because efficiency brings more prosperity. Sons and daughters leave home for universities and "greener pastures." The elements of cohesion become strained, and we can see the social consequences.

There is no point in yearning for the rural village, the oxen and plow. They are not the essence of tradition; they were born of necessity. But our family feels a commitment to support those who retain the core values. We know people for whom handmade production is the essence of their livelihood, such as those who weave esparto grass, or others who carve bowls of solid pieces of olive wood.

Others have adapted age-old procedures to bring quality products to more people. I think of the Gil brothers producing fine wine from the rocky soil of Jumilla, or Belén, who has made her hand-painted Puente ceramics dishwasher safe.

My family and I have been nourished by the special gifts the people of Spain have brought to our lives over the years. As I introduce you to Miguel, Lola, Jorge, and many other Spaniards in my reflections, it is my hope that you also will be enriched by their stories of lives filled with generosity and integrity.

"The general opinion was that he was a saint."

Don Ignacio:
The Spirit of Generosity

I begin this collection of essays with a portrait of a Spanish gentleman, Don Ignacio Millán, whose life personified the virtues of goodness and hospitality. I find in him the embodiment of all that is noble in the Spanish soul. To this day my abiding image of this humble man is of him serving a simple meal to young American sailors on a spiritual retreat. Some of them were young enough to have been his great-grandchildren, yet they were his honored guests.

Don Ignacio was a frail, ascetic nobleman born in the nineteenth century. It was hard to tell an exact age when looking into the face of one who had endured first the religious persecution of the 1920s; then the hunger and devastation of the Spanish Civil War, where almost one third of the male population was slain; and finally the deprivation of World War II and its aftermath of political and economic isolation.

I first met Don Ignacio in 1973 at his bedside in Villa Ballena—the House of the Whale. I was with my good friend Pedro Díaz. We were looking for a site to hold the weekend retreats I would lead as a chaplain stationed at the Naval Base in Rota. Pedro was a warm and expansive man with a great love for Americans. You can read more about him in my essay titled "The Shoemaker's Son and Carpenter's Daughter."

Villa Ballena was an unpretentious but elegant retreat house located on the beach of Chipiona. At that time, it was a modest fishing village. We heard waves lapping at the base of the pre-Christian lighthouse nearby as we approached the door of Don Ignacio's dwelling. Beyond the lighthouse the surf was swelling over remnants of stone Phoenician fish traps near its base.

Bundled up for the chilling winds, Pedro and I rapped on the glass pane of the villa's front door. A widow dressed in traditional black for mourning came to the door. When we told her our mission, she led us to a bedroom at the end of the main tile-clad corridor.

The frail figure of Don Ignacio, suffering from influenza, rose from his sick bed and bowed graciously. "You are especially welcome," he said humbly, "I will forever be grateful for the Americans who brought food to our little town of Chipiona when we were hungry."

After we described the purpose of our visit, without hesitation Don Ignacio offered me Villa Ballena as the site for Credo Weekends. He said that all he wanted was one dollar per person for the four-day retreat! As he bid us goodbye he said, "I am honored to have an opportunity to give back what we have received."

The villa has an interesting history. As was the custom for young men of means, Don Ignacio and his brother were privileged to attend the month-long Ejercicios Espirituales—the Spiritual Exercises of Ignacio de Loyola. The Millán brothers were so moved by the experience that they vowed to extend the blessing they received to the less fortunate fishermen of the town. Sparing no expense, Don Ignacio joined with his brother, an architect, to build Villa Ballena.

As he welcomed the American sailors, marines and members of their families into his house during the ensuing months, Don Ignacio could see his dream fulfilled in another way. Once more, he was helping common seafaring people in their search for the love of God and new life.

Two widows, Rosario and Catalina, prepared simple and hearty meals for the sailors. Don Ignacio, wearing a vest and black bowtie typical of local waiters, served the sailors elegantly. Sometimes between meals, the aged gentleman would slip out and drive to Sevilla seventy miles away, where he would visit the elderly folks who lived in another structure that he and his brother had built to serve their less fortunate pensioners. Of course, many of the residents were younger than he.

Don Ignacio insisted upon only one thing: that the name of each Navy guest would be entered in a ledger listing all those who went on retreat at Villa Ballena over the years. At the end of each retreat, after they had rolled up their sleeping bags to prepare for their return to the base, each sailor and Marine would pause by a small table where frail Don Ignacio sat with his timeworn register. With a sense of deep satisfaction evident to all, the holy man entered their names alongside hundreds of Spaniards who had come before.

Once, he told me how impressed he was that the American young people showed such seriousness during the retreat, wistfully observing that this was not always the case with modern Spanish youth. As we walked along the beach one day, I asked Don Ignacio whether he had ever been married. He looked into my face with a twinkle in his eyes and answered, "Who would ever want to marry me? I give away all that I have."

Indeed this was so, for as the years passed, he even offered to give me Villa Ballena as a permanent residence for ministry to the Naval Base. Tempting as the offer was, I was not at a point in my journey where I could consider such a radical move.

A few years later, I tried to contact Don Ignacio in Sevilla. I received the following handwritten note.

> I write you to communicate with all regrets and deep feelings that unfortunately, and surely because God wanted him by His side, seven months ago, the good and saintly Don Ignacio died. He has left a trail of good deeds behind that all of us will never forget. He was a man of exemplary conduct, sharing, humble, charitable, diligent, generous, modest, virtuous. If you knew him I suppose it is unnecessary to continue listing his praises. The general opinion was that he was a saint.

Subsequently Don Ignacio's grace-filled structure, Villa Ballena, fell to the wrecker's ball to make room for another anonymous beachfront condominium. I returned eighteen years later with my son Jonathan and could not find a trace.

But does that really matter? Thirty years later, the light of Don Ignacio's generosity and humility abides with me, and with many of the sailors and marines who had the privilege of knowing him. Don Ignacio's life is a reminder that the acts of kindness and generosity you express toward others have a life of their own. You make it a better place for all of us.

¡Que rico!

1

Food, Culture, and Friends

Plaza del Cabildo, Sanlúcar de Barrameda (Cádiz)

Sharing a Meal
Nourishing the Spirit

When my wife Ruth and I entered a Spanish restaurant for the first time, we gained a key insight about the Spanish people. As the waiter was seating us, others in the dining room looked up from their meals and quietly greeted us. Throughout the time we were eating, people said goodbye to everyone in the dining room as they finished their meals and went on their way.

This routine—almost a ritual—of acknowledging one another when dining in a restaurant is an example of the intimacy of interchange that is the defining characteristic of the Spanish people. They seem to be saying to one another, "We are all in this life together, with our common needs—why not enjoy each other's company?"

To the Spaniard, eating is far more than the process of satisfying hunger ("putting on the feed-bag," as my mother would jokingly say). Spaniards take dining seriously. Several times in the course of a day, they pause to eat with colleagues or family members. Dining in Spain is a shared experience even though individuals are eating at their separate tables.

When I was young and foolish, I was convinced that when touring Spain one needed to be efficient. There were so many wonderful things to see, and so little time: countryside villages, Roman ruins, and pilgrimage churches. We would investigate one town in the morning; then stop by the local market to buy some fresh bread, cheese and a bottle of wine for a quick picnic by the side of the road. In twenty minutes, we would be on our way to the next destination, zipping along byways that were free of traffic. No more dodging slow and noisy trucks—the drivers were having dinner and a little siesta.

It seemed that everyone in the countryside had stopped what they were doing and were having a leisurely meal together! I thought to myself, "What an enormous expenditure of time, when there are so many things to see and do." I later realized that I was missing the essence of Spain.

Visigothic churches may be fascinating, and brooding castles may be remarkable, but a leisurely dinner among Spaniards was far more important if we wished to know Spain and her people. In some circumstances, efficiency may be a virtue—but not to the traditional Spaniard—particularly if it is going to compromise the quality of his life.

The food normally eaten in restaurants is nothing flamboyant or pretentious, just good, fresh food prepared from local recipes. It is a straightforward and honest expression of the region in which it is prepared. With seventeen autonomous regions, there are an infinite variety of dishes. Celtic Galicia serves wonderful caldos—stews in pots bubbling with leeks, garlic, ham, chunks of beef and pork, kale, collards and potatoes. Or we could be eating paella or arroz a banda in the Mediterranean port of Valencia, where its long Moorish immersion is reflected in age-old recipes with rice and saffron.

What I find remarkable today is that the New Spain, with all of these venerable region-specific cuisines under her belt, is now in the vanguard of European cuisine. It seems as if traditional Spain's various culinary threads have been woven into a tapestry that the whole world admires!

The next time you grab a bite to eat and hurry on your way, remember that dining is also a time for the refreshment of your spirit in the company of others. That sense of companionship is central to the traditional way of life in Spain, and the people are richer for it.

Harvests of the New World

When I was a little boy, I once lay on my bed with a coloring book propped on the pillow. It was a delightful publication with a Thanksgiving harvest theme. On the center pages, I found the outline of a cornucopia—a horn of plenty—burgeoning with all kinds of fruits of the soil. I had so much fun filling in the drawing with varied colors, using my twelve-color Crayola box. Those were the days before the sixty-four crayon cartons featuring colors such "Macaroni & Cheese" and "Purple Mountain Majesty."

Harvest has always been a satisfying season for me. I see in each fruit and vegetable the fulfillment of their growth from spring seedlings to autumn maturity. Locally, my grandchildren get a hint of this view of life when they make their annual visit to "Pumpkinville"—a field of haystacks and long vines that harbor big orange jack o' lanterns.

Over the years, Ruth and I have often traveled through the Spanish countryside during the autumn months. Some villages were fragrant with the aroma of wine during their Vendimia wine festival celebration. In the valley of La Vera, among the cherry trees and farms, we visited with the farmers who were preparing smoked paprika. They were slowly curing freshly picked peppers over smoldering oak stumps in smoke houses. Two weeks later the peppers would be ready for the mill that would produce the brilliant red powder of unique pimentón de La Vera—a standard item in any Spanish kitchen, and a key ingredient in chorizo.

One might imagine a timeless Spain, with local harvest traditions that have been going on for thousands of years. But of course this is not the case. Radical changes occurred in 1492: the final triumph of the 700-year struggle with the Moors on the plains of Granada, and more notably, Christopher Columbus's discovery of America. It was a watershed for Spain and its cuisine. The

Another New World gift: piquillo peppers arriving from the farm in Lodosa (La Rioja)

introduction of new foods from the Americas heralded a revolution in how Spaniards farmed, cooked and enjoyed food.

King Fernando and Queen Isabel sent Columbus in search of rare spices. Seasonings such as black pepper were so precious that the monarchs hoped his voyage would discover a new route to the Spice Islands. Why were spices so crucial? Remember they did not have side-by-side refrigerators providing an unlimited supply of ice cubes to tumble into their glasses of Coca Cola. They had no refrigeration at all. Pepper, along with sea salt, was a priceless preservative for their meats.

When Columbus returned from the New World, he headed straight to the Royal Court, which at the time was encamped at the Real Monasterio de Guadalupe deep in the mountains of Cáceres of western Spain. (Fernando and Isabel had an itinerant court that was often on the move in order to reinforce relationships across various parts of their realm.) In the monastery Columbus presented his patrons with chili peppers, gold, and other treasures. The king and queen were delighted, particularly by the new foods.

The local Franciscan brothers sowed the pepper seeds in the monastery gardens—less than a day's journey from where smoked paprika is produced today! From that time forward people on both continents have enjoyed food that was flavored and preserved by smoked paprika, thanks to the horticultural interest of Columbus.

The many other culinary treasures that the first explorers brought back to Spain were far more lasting than silver and gold. They changed the way of life for all of Europe. The list of foodstuffs is amazing: vanilla, chocolate, tomatoes, potatoes, squash, corn, avocado, pineapples, and peppers of all sorts. Where would we be without them?

The Spaniards also introduced many of their treasures to America. Can you imagine a time when there were no citrus fruits in California, Texas and Florida? Imagine the Wild West without horses? Explorers and missionaries brought them all to the New World. Since Spaniards have always loved good food, Christopher Columbus made sure some ibérico pigs were included on the first voyage. After all, how could a Spaniard properly dine without his pata negra ham? In the next two years, the herd grew to 300. Believe it or not, descendants of these pigs now reside here in Colonial Williamsburg, Virginia!

When you next sit down at your Thanksgiving table, surrounded by family and other loved ones, don't forget the intrepid forebears who contributed to the food before you—a cornucopia of many civilizations.

Local churrería in Cádiz

Chocolate:
Should Cupid Play Castanets?

I don't necessarily think that Cupid should be playing castanets, but I do know that it is due to Christopher Columbus and Hernán Cortés that you can give a gift of chocolate to your loved one on St. Valentine's Day.

Cacao is a product largely grown in the Amazon rain forests of Ecuador and Venezuela. The use of chocolate as a beverage progressed via the Mayans and the Olmecs of Central America to the Aztecs and finally the Spaniards. Every day Emperor Montezuma drank fifty or more golden goblets of chocolate, and it was ritually used at betrothal and wedding ceremonies. Chocolate was thought to be an aphrodisiac. (Maybe that's where Cupid got the idea.)

Spaniards have been enthralled with chocolate since 1544. It was then that Dominican friars, accompanied by Mayans from Guatemala, presented containers of ready-to-drink frothed chocolate to young Prince Philip, soon to be Philip II. He and his entourage were enchanted.

Soon, any Spanish nobleman worth his salt reconfigured his house to have a chocolate room—usually situated between the Large Hall and the drawing room. In such a room, as a man of leisure, Philip would spend hours in pleasant conversation with significant friends. However, as a pious Catholic he was faced with a troubling dilemma: he found that a cup of chocolate assuaged his hunger while he was fasting. If the Church classified chocolate as a beverage he was within bounds, for beverages were not included in the rules of fasting. However if chocolate was considered a food, then he would be deprived of chocolate during Lent and other holy days throughout the liturgical year. His confessor assured the scrupulous Philip that drinking chocolate was exempt from fasting requirements.

Chocolate a la taza—Thick hot chocolate with hot churros (Zamora)

A Good Friday treat in Zamora

The young king eventually moved the capital of Spain from Toledo to Madrid, and by the 1620s the city's population numbered about 130,000 people. Believe it or not, the new city had more than 350 tons of cacao and chocolate in shops and warehouses.

Spaniards and Portuguese consumed phenomenal amounts of chocolate for the next hundred years, while the rest of Europe was completely unaware of this new food. Chocolate sweet shops called chocolaterías sprang up throughout the Iberian Peninsula, and by the nineteenth century one third of the world's entire cacao production was consumed by Spaniards.

As chocolate spread beyond Spain, the country's European possessions moved to the forefront of chocolate production—especially the Spanish Netherlands (present-day Holland and Belgium).

Chocolate has also had military uses. Olmecs, Aztecs, and later, Spanish soldiers were issued wafers of cacao, which they would consume for extra strength during marches and in battle. One of history's coincidences is that five hundred years later during the First World War the American army included three four-ounce chocolate bars in a soldier's "D-Ration" for much the same purpose.

During World War II virtually all U.S. chocolate production was requisitioned for the military. Although the purpose of the available chocolate was to sustain our men in battle, liberating American GIs generously shared their chocolate with hungry children in Europe. Chocolate bars became associated with the return of peace and normalcy.

The next time you are in Madrid be sure to visit a fabled chocolatería located next to the Church of San Ginés, in the neighborhood of Puerta del Sol. The street level has a charming nineteenth-century bar with white marble tables. Even today, well over one hundred years later, this magical place is filled to the brim with people of all ages enjoying chocolate a la taza (thick hot chocolate in which one dips churros). The Chocolatería San Ginés is never closed, and is especially busy in the early evening after work. There is standing room only from four in the morning onward, to the delight of "night owls" who are wrapping up their all-night revelry!

Tempting pimientos de Padrón in a cazuela

The Legend of Padrón

Contemporary culture seems to be very receptive to fantasy and legend. There is great interest in the legend of the Holy Grail, Tolkien's *Middle Earth*, C.S. Lewis's *Narnia* and J.K. Rowling's *Harry Potter*. The latest and greatest roller-coaster at Busch Gardens is named after a mythological beast, the gryphon. I wonder how many of you realize that the wonderful little pimientos de Padrón are also wrapped in legend! Although there is no parallel with the enthusiasm about Harry Potter, each year we ask our local Virginia farmer to plant a few more rows of seedlings.

The origin of the seeds from which we grow these delightful peppers traces back to a rustic town along the Atlantic coast of Galicia, in farthest northwest Spain. The town of Padrón is so far west that the neighboring village on the storm-tossed Atlantic Coast is called Finisterre—loosely translated as "Land's End."

Padrón is shrouded in history and legend that stretch back to pre-history. Archeologists tell us that it was an Iberian settlement of the Caporos people. Because of its natural location at the confluence of two rivers, the settlement was on the crossroads to what is now Braga (Portugal) to the south and Astorga (León) to the east. Classical Roman documents indicate that it became a significant town named Iria Flavia under the Romans.

Here is where the need to sort out history and legend comes into play. According to tradition, it was in a rocky area above Iria Flavia that Apostle Saint James first preached during his stay in Hispania. Spain was at the peak of its cultural ascendency in the Roman Empire, so it is conceivable that James would head there, as had St. Paul, according to Biblical accounts.

Unfortunately he returned to the Holy Land, where he was martyred in Jerusalem. His disciples Theodore and Athanasius placed the body of James in a stone boat and sailed westward. They navigated the mythical stone craft across the expanse of the Mediterranean Sea, traveled by Gibraltar through the Pillars of Hercules, and headed north along the Iberian coast until they found safe haven in a peaceful ría or fjord. There they moored their stone vessel to a pedrón (Spanish for big stone).

The two disciples remained in Iria Flavia (now Padrón—Patron) to preach after burying the body of the apostle in Compostela. The legendary pedrón mooring stone can be seen today at the parish church of Santiago de Padrón.

Legend has it that some shepherds in a field saw a star shining on the site of St. James's grave in Compostela. It was during the final throes of the eighth-century struggle against the invading Moors. As news of the shepherd's miraculous discovery spread to the defending armies they took heart, and at the critical battle of Covadonga, they saw St. James riding out of heaven on a splendid white charger in order to lead the Spaniards to victory. For more on this story, read the essay "Covadonga: Tales of War and Cheese."

Padrón soon became a popular passing place in the Camino de Santiago pilgrimage route, but the focus of attention gradually moved to nearby

Compostela, capital of Galicia. Here is where the peppers come in (you thought I had forgotten).

Over the years a Franciscan monastery grew up in the barrio of Herbón, a neighborhood of Padrón. At the Herbón monastery, Franciscans first grew the pepper seeds they had brought back from the New World in the eighteenth century. This place remains the heart of the pimientos de Padrón belt today.

A member of the La Tienda community wrote,

> I am from Padrón—my family originates from there. We have a 100-year-old farmhouse next to the monastery in Herbón, the small village contained in Padrón. All my aunties and uncles produce these pimientos. There is also an annual fiesta to celebrate the pimiento. People come from all around to visit.

What do these legends and fantasies have to do with the very tasty and occasionally hot tiny green peppers? Had the Spaniards not believed the legend of Santiago, they might easily have lost the crucial Battle of Covadonga to the surging invaders. Hispania would have had a radically different culture, in which Franciscans could not flourish, nor could they plant peppers in their monasteries. Nor would there be the pilgrims to Santiago de Compostela to enjoy them in their tapas bars, and therefore the fame of the peppers would never have spread across Spain and the world.

Are these stories true? Could a stone ship sail across the Mediterranean? Was the body the shepherds found really that of St. James or just another first century Roman? How could the soldiers have seen James riding out of heaven on a white horse? These are questions that we as benighted children of the scientific age ask. Certainly they would not have occurred to a medieval pilgrim. For him, life was a mystery.

So when next you sauté in olive oil your portion of these unique peppers which originated in Galicia, and when you dust them with sea salt before popping them into your mouth as a delightful tapa, be thankful for those whose trusting naiveté has enabled you to savor a unique treat from far western Spain.

Los Maragatos:
A Thousand Years of History

My family has covered the byways of Spain for over forty years—first just Ruth and I, then traveling with our children, and in recent years our adult sons with their families. In other essays I share with you some of our personal encounters with families. I hope they give you a window into Spain's rich and complex culture. In the section "Local Artisans," you will read about Pepe from Murcia, who is the maestro of paella rice. Or José and Amalia, who produce artisan peppers and other vegetables from the ancient kingdom of Navarra. You will also meet Jorge, the irrepressible shepherd of wine.

Later in this section, I will introduce you to Antonio, a jovial scholar and gourmand, who teaches at the University of Cáceres.

But before then I would like you to meet my friend Esteban, whose family roots go back almost 1,000 years. He is a warm and gentle man whom our family has met on several occasions.

Esteban and his brother Javier work with his father, Esteban Salvadores, who founded a small business, El Maragato. The business is located in the ancient stone village of Castrillo de los Polvazares, which was first an encampment of the Roman legion. In medieval times villagers welcomed pilgrims traveling along the Camino de Santiago.

The Salvadores family take great pride in their fabas, Granja Asturiana— the legendary fabada beans grown for centuries in the neighboring kingdom of Asturias. La Granja beans from Asturias are the crucial ingredients for authentic fabada, the bean and sausage stew which has been emblematic of the Asturias for over one thousand years. La Granja beans are unique because they have an uncanny ability to absorb the complex tastes that chorizo and black sausage lend to the broth, in much the same way as bomba rice does in paella.

Production of fabas de la Granja is extremely limited because they need to be planted and weeded by hand along the fertile valleys and riverbanks of Asturias. They take 150 days to mature, in contrast to ordinary beans, which take ninety days. They have to be hand tied to the vines, hand husked, and then dried in raised stone barns called horreos. As with many of the finest products of Spain, there is no substitute for individual attention—you need to follow centuries-old procedures.

Esteban and his family could not be more rooted in the history and culture of Spain. They are direct descendants of the enigmatic people known as the Maragatos. In medieval Spain these men established trading networks so that goods or gold could be transported safely.

The national epic, "El Poema de Mio Cid," gives evidence that the Maragatos were entrusted by El Cid and the court of King Alfonso VI of León to

Castrillo de los Polvazares (León)

transport his daughters' dowry as well as riches gained from El Cid's conquest of the Moors in Valencia and Alicante. One transfer involved more than 200 horses!

Three hundred years later, Esteban's Maragato ancestors were indispensable during the reign of King Fernando and Queen Isabel. Commissioned by the Catholic Kings, "Los Reyes Católicos," they transported munitions through the rugged mountains to aid in the reconquest of Granada in 1492. In recognition of their contribution to Christian Spain's liberation, his family was given a title of nobility and was known locally as the "Salvadores de Castrillo" (Saviors from Castrillo). Salvadores is still their surname today!

These are the historical and cultural roots of Esteban and his family—early traders and people of commerce. What a privilege it is to listen to him as he proudly recounts how his grandfather and great grandfather were very much of the tradition of their Maragato forebears.

He describes how they traveled throughout northern Spain from Galicia to Navarra and Huesca trading wines, oil, dried goods, bacalao and other salted meats and fish (salazones).

Over time dried goods and particularly beans became the backbone of their enterprise, since they were easier to haul and store than salazones, and weighed far less than wines. Following family tradition (how could he not?) Esteban's father founded the present-day company, El Maragato, and is now working with his two unmarried sons. (At La Tienda I have a similar sense of satisfaction working with my sons—but Ruth and I have been blessed with even more—four frisky grandchildren!)

Esteban says that they chose the name El Maragato for their business because it suggests honesty and evokes a sense of continuity. (It was not that long ago when mule trains transported goods such as beans.) But most of all, the name was chosen because the Salvadores family is proud of their cultural and historical roots as full-blooded Maragatos. To demonstrate their commitment to their community, they have included a beech wood spoon with many of the bags, made by handicapped people in their village.

Ruth has been reading *The Bible in Spain*, an account by nineteenth-century English linguist and traveler George Borrow, about his travels in Spain. You might enjoy reading it. In this fascinating memoir, the author wrote:

In a word, almost the entire commerce of nearly one half of Spain passes through the hands of the Maragatos, whose fidelity to their trust is such, that no one accustomed to employ them would hesitate to confide to them the transport of a ton of treasure from the sea of Biscay to Madrid; knowing well that it would not be their fault were it not delivered safe and undiminished, even of a grain, and that bold must be the thieves who would seek to wrest it from the far feared Maragatos, who would cling to it whilst they could stand, and would cover it with their bodies when they fell in the act of loading or discharging their long carbines.

When we first met Esteban we were attracted to the quality of his artisan products. We had no idea that we would have the honor of working with such a solid and noble family, deeply rooted in the traditions of Spain. They reflect Spain's best.

Manchego:
The Treasure of La Mancha

Let me tell you of a happy coincidence that led my family to find one of the very finest manchego cheeses in Spain. A few years ago, our sons Tim and Jonathan had finished visiting small producers in the south of Spain, and decided to return to Madrid via Extremadura, along the Portuguese border. After driving for several hours, they approached Trujillo, one of our favorite towns. It was now late in the afternoon, and they wanted to stretch their legs.

For as long as people can remember, Trujillo has held a cheese competition in the plaza mayor, which is surrounded by ancient, splendid stone buildings. There are always cheeses from rural producers who come from all over Spain: local ones such as the fabled torta del casar with its rich creamy interior, and even some cheeses from as far away as Galicia, Catalunya or the Balearic Island of Minorca.

Producers are drawn to Trujillo because of this historic fair's reputation. Those people include manchego cheese producers from distant La Mancha. There are many cheeses called "manchego," just as there are many cheeses called "cheddar." Some that you will find in the supermarket are industrial cheeses and taste fine. Other cheeses, hand-made by artisans, are finer. They capture the truly artisan tradition. Thereby hangs my tale.

Jonathan and Tim strolled around many displays of the artisan cheeses of Spain, and happened by the stand of a warm and pleasant man named Antonio Villajos. He and his assistant Raúl were very excited because their tiny family operation had just won the prize for producing the finest manchego in Spain. It was a particularly remarkable accomplishment because Antonio and

Handmade, award-winning manchego from the Villajos brothers

his brothers Vicente and Julián only started bringing their homemade cheese
to market in 1996!

As my sons sampled the prize-winning cheese, they were convinced that
this was indeed a remarkable manchego. Even better, the hand-made cheese
was made by a small family producer—the kind of people La Tienda is committed to support.

Now for a little background: true manchego cheese comes only from sheep
of the manchega strain. Thousands of years ago, wild sheep crossed the Pyrenees and migrated through various parts of Spain such as Aragón and Castilla
y León. Eventually they settled in the high plateau region of La Mancha, southeast of Madrid. La Mancha (the Moors called it Al-Mansha "dry land") is a high
plain, 600–700 meters in altitude, with intense and bitter winters. The sheep
have remained on the land of La Mancha until the present time.

Iberian archeological sites confirm that the earliest residents of this vast, rolling countryside domesticated the manchega sheep. Through skillful breeding they improved the stock, without allowing the breed to mix with other kinds of sheep. The manchega sheep's unique characteristics have hardly changed through the centuries. Their thick wool, grown to resist the cold winters, and their remarkably rich milk are legendary.

These hardy sheep live most of their natural life outdoors, as they have for centuries. All year long free-range herds of manchega sheep roam the countryside, foraging among the sparse herbs and grasses. Today, shepherds enrich the ewes' (female sheep) diet during their pregnancy.

The terrain of this sheep country is dotted with small villages of hardly more than a main street. There are houses on each side of the street, and family ranches stretch into the countryside. The Villajos brothers make their classic cheese in the remote town of Porzuna, nestled in the hills close to the Montes de Toledo in the Province of Ciudad Real. In what was originally their family home, they produce a handcrafted cheese. It is made from the fresh raw milk collected from a few local farmers whose manchega sheep graze on the pastures nearby.

The key to their cheese is the skilled hand of master cheese maker Beni. Each small batch made from their rich milk is sampled by a representative of the Denomination of Origin board to certify that it is 100% manchega sheep's milk and is aged for a minimum of ninety days.

The rinds of these cheeses have the signature herringbone pattern, a legacy of the pattern traditionally imprinted by the woven esparto grass mats used to mould the cheeses. The exterior varies in color from white to yellow. They are never waxed or colored, as are industrial cheeses.

It was a fortuitous chain of events that enabled us to bring to your table an extraordinary manchego cheese that has earned four Gran Selección prizes in the past five years! It is a remarkable achievement to win so many of these esteemed awards during such a short term.

What a happy coincidence that Tim and Jonathan stopped to stretch their legs in Trujillo!

Membrillo

Christmas Confections and Suffering Quince

I am intrigued by paradoxes in human behavior—history is full of them. One of the most delicious of these (in many senses of the word) is that the traditional cakes and confections that Spaniards enjoy every Christmas have their roots in the Moorish culture of Spain.

The Biblical staples of almonds and honey are at the core of Middle East cuisine. To this day honey is a major focus of commerce in that region. The Moors brought the almond tree with them to Spain. Most Christmas confections enjoyed in Spain—whether it is turrón from Alicante, mazapán from Toledo, or polvorones and roscones from Córdoba, are made of almonds or honey.

The centrality of the almond in daily Spanish life was illustrated to us when several years ago we set out to have the finest mantecados for Christmas. We wanted the best in Spain, and the little town of Estepa, deep in the countryside of Córdoba, was reputed to be the source. At first we thought it would be easy to get them.

We emailed an order to the producer in July so that they could deliver the products to our shipping container in a timely manner, well in time for the busy holiday season. We believe in planning ahead. Well, we waited and waited for a reply. After a month passed we decided to telephone them, but to no avail. Finally, in October we established contact—so much for our advanced planning for shipments to the States.

The following spring Ruth and I decided to visit the town of Estepa, the historic center of polvorones in Spain. We wanted to get a flavor of the place, and to meet the management of the company we contacted, so that we could understand exactly what was going on. The owners of this family company greeted us cordially and proudly showed us around their bakery. To our surprise, there was virtually no activity in the plant. In fact, the town of Estepa seemed especially laid back, with a pace of life that we can only envy.

Then we discovered the secret. Life in Estepa is directly affected by the almond harvest. Other than preparing and maintaining the facilities, there is nothing to be done until the trucks full of fresh almonds roll into town in September. At that moment, the whole community springs into action. Men bring the almonds to the processing area. Their wives set aside normal home-making tasks and head for the huge bakery. For the next several weeks, they work together to produce the famous confections that will grace thousands of homes throughout Spain.

Many of the cookies are very fragile. Polvorones get their name because they may crumble in your hand, turning to a sweet nutty powder. In fact many Spaniards crumble them before eating them. They are a combination of ground almonds, honey and Ibérico shortening—so delicate that they are individually hand wrapped in tissue paper for their protection. The same care is given to the crunchier roscones, small doughnut-shaped almond cookies flavored with wine, as well as alfajores, a spiced almond shortbread traditionally from Sevilla. As you can see, the almond is king.

If we move east of Córdoba toward the Mediterranean, we encounter the province of Alicante and the small town of Jijona where tons of almonds are delivered each autumn. The almond is key to producing artisan-quality turrón—which is nothing but almonds and honey, with the addition of a little egg white for the crunchier "Alicante" version. The softer "Jijona" turrón is like its Middle Eastern cousin, halvah, except it is made from ground almonds rather than ground sesame seeds. In Spain, Christmas is not Christmas without turrón!

We learned about a couple of other cherished holiday confections when we visited the medieval walled city of Ávila—far from sunny Andalucía. We met the owner of the esteemed Yemas de Santa Teresa. He makes yemas, a medieval confection made of egg yolk that is dropped into hot sugar syrup.

He also makes what is purported to be the finest membrillo (quince preserve) in Spain. As he was talking to us he apologized, because although he still makes his famous membrillo from the traditional recipe, demand has grown so much that he has started to augment his supply of quince with some grown in Chile.

"The quince fruit of Spain have to endure the vicissitudes of winter," he explained, "whereas the fruit from Chile matures in a climate of perpetual summer. Therefore they are not the same—the ripening quinces of Chile have had it too easy." He looked at me intently and said, "If you have not suffered, you are silly!" How very Spanish of him, I thought. I do not know about suffering quinces, but he was expressing a truth: that through struggle and testing you become a more mature person. I never expected a philosophical twist to a discussion of membrillo!

At any rate, I asked him about importing his celebrated mazapán, one of the greatest of all Christmas treats. He replied, regretfully, that it was not possible to ship it to America, because authentic mazapán has a shelf life of only a few days. The combination of ingredients is so fragile that the jostling and temperature changes of shipment would ruin it. We heard the same story from the most famous mazapán producer in Toledo, who adamantly refuses to sell us his product, even when we offer to ship it by air, as we have done with our polvorones and mantecados. So, if you are an epicure, you will have to wait until your next trip to Spain to enjoy the finest expression of mazapán.

Antonio Gázquez:
The Professor of Jamón

I would like to introduce you to a remarkable person, Antonio Gázquez Ortiz. He is a man of extraordinary breadth: scholar, author, research scientist, and renowned gastronome. He is also a man of depth, a father, and a friend with a generous heart. He and his wife Purificación have two adult sons: David, 27, a professor of music and Miguel Ángel, 21, who is a photographer, designer and musician. They also have three daughters: Puri, 22, a university student; Yia, 21, who is married and Lola, 10, who is in primary school.

Antonio represents the best of Extremadura—one of the most appealing regions of Spain. In addition the stately Cáceres, I particularly enjoy the village of Trujillo, home of many conquistadores, and the shrine of Nuestra Señora de Guadalupe, a favorite of King Fernando and Queen Isabel.

The region is the home of ranchers and breeders of the fabled black-hoofed Ibérico pigs that have made this land their habitat for centuries. These animals are the source of the celebrated jamón ibérico, and provided the impetus for our ten-year quest to bring this precious product to the tables of America. You can read more about them in the next essay, "Ibérico: The Romance of the Frontier."

The search for the fabled ham has taken our family along many paths in these southwestern reaches of Spain. Ruth and I made a pilgrimage to the village of Jabugo in western Andalucía, and much later to the Pedroches Dehesa pastureland north of Córdoba. On other trips, my sons Tim, Jonathan and I have been privileged to meet some of the most famous producers of jamón ibérico in the ham city of Guijuelo. We also met a producer in the rugged mountain village of La Alberca, also located in the province of Salamanca.

But it was when we met Antonio Gázquez in Cáceres that our experiences coalesced. And what better place to meet him than in ancient and noble Cáceres? Romans founded the city in the first century. It weathered barbarian and Moorish invasions, and then regained its original splendor when the returning conquistadors built señorial houses within its walls. During all these changes wrought by men, the black-hoofed pigs were minding their business, fattening up on delicious acorns from the local cork and holm oak trees. Perhaps we can learn something from them!

Before moving on with my story, I must tell you a little more about Cáceres. It presents excellent examples of two very different parts of its heritage— the Moorish fortress and the Gothic city. Because of its remote location, the citizens have been able to preserve and promote one of the most complete Medieval and Renaissance quarters in the world. Coats of arms adorn the palaces and ancestral homes inhabited by noble families.

The beauty and appeal of Cáceres comes from immersing yourself in the labyrinth of streets and tiny plazas, passing under arches, past towers and walls, between churches, beautiful convents and innumerable palaces. You will discover an incredible mix of architectural design ranging from Moorish to Northern Gothic to the Italian Renaissance. The Parador (country inn) in Cáceres is set on the Moorish foundations of the Torreorgaz Palace. With all of this to see, and hardly a random tourist in sight, Cáceres offers a wonderful way to move away from the twenty-first century and enjoy the relative peace of another era.

But let's get back to Dr Gázquez. His roots are in the soil of Extremadura. It is there that he has devoted his life to unraveling and expounding upon the myth of the ibérico pig, which has roamed the Iberian Peninsula from the time of the cave men. Holding the chair of histology (the study of animal tissues) at the University of Extremadura in Cáceres, he has approached these legendary animals with pure scientific analysis. Dr Gázquez has inspired many of his students to continue the search for greater understanding of this unique animal.

My sons Tim and Jonathan, friend Jamie and I were traveling through the region in order to learn as much as we could about this fabled pig, often

My son Tim with Antonio Gázquez enjoying an afternoon with noble cerdos ibéricos

referred to as pata negra. My friend Peter Kaminsky, a writer for the *New York Times*, told me of his experience with Antonio while doing research for his fascinating book, *Pig Perfect*. After reading this book, I resolved to meet the man about whom Peter spoke so highly. We contacted Dr. Gázquez by email. I received an enthusiastic reply from him, suggesting that we meet at a café on the outskirts of Cáceres.

When we arrived at the roadside café that morning we were greeted warmly by Antonio and his rancher companion. We got to know one another a bit while enjoying churros and café con leche, and then set out in two vehicles to explore a nearby ranch where ibérico pigs were being raised. In one car, my sons soon became lost in animated conversation with Antonio about animal husbandry. My friend Jamie and I were in the other car with the rancher, a cordial and knowledgeable gentleman who told us all there was to know about the practical concerns of raising these remarkable animals.

After we rejoined and met the pigs at a waterhole, it was time for the traditional Spanish mid-day meal. I would not call it a lunch; I would call it a feast. The Spanish know how to break bread together. As we left for our meal, the pigs glanced at us with only passing interest. Their feast would come in the autumn when the surrounding acres of cork oaks would provide them with an abundance of bellotas (tasty acorns).

Antonio took us to the medieval section of Cáceres with its narrow streets and stone battlements. Adjacent to the handsome cobble-stoned Plaza de San Juan was Antonio's favorite restaurant, El Figón de Eustaquio. The venerable building, with dark wood paneling, was filled with expectant diners and skilled waiters darting from table to table. As we were ushered to an elegant private dining room in back, we passed by the kitchen from which came aromas of roast meat and herbs.

At the dinner table Antonio the professor was transformed into Antonio the gastronome as he presided over a sumptuous feast. Before us were local cheeses, fresh shellfish, wines, and plates of paper-thin sliced jamón ibérico that glistened in the warmth of the room. Jamón's monounsaturated marbling turns to liquid at 70° F—truly extraordinary! In a genuine and unassuming way, Antonio acquainted us with the fine art of enjoying the fruits of the earth.

Antonio Gázquez is a man for all seasons. A genuine enthusiast, he enjoys being an author, a gourmet, a scientist and a historian. Most of all, he loves to teach. He has written many scholarly articles and books, some of which are the definitive texts in his field. Three recent books are particularly engaging: *Porcus, Puerco, Cerdo*—a history of the pig in Spanish gastronomy, *La Cocina en Tiempos del Arcipreste de Hita*—an account of the medieval cuisine of Christians, Jews and Moors, and *Conversations with a Gastronome,* where he reflects on the cuisine of late twentieth century.

I was impressed with the knowledge and grace of this man. It was a privilege to be in his company.

Ibérico:
The Romance of the Western Frontier

Ruth and I began our serious exploration of Spain in 1965, when the country was beginning to stir from a long social and economic slumber. The years of poverty brought on by the Civil War and its aftermath were still a fresh memory. Many mothers of Spain were dressed in black. In much of Spain the "moto" (motor bike) was the only mode of transportation if one chose not to walk.

In those days, Ruth and I would rent a small SEAT 600—the most basic of cars—and set off into the countryside. We particularly liked heading west beyond Salamanca toward the western border with Portugal, where traces of modernity are less apparent. In the midst of this mountainous part of Salamanca, among the craggy landscape of rocks and meadows, is the dehesa, a grassy pastureland dotted with cork and holm oaks.

The dehesa is the favorite grazing area of the free-range black-hoofed cerdo ibérico, the rare ibérico pig. During the autumn, each one of them gobbles up bellotas (acorns) fallen from the trees at the astonishing rate of over twenty pounds of acorns a day! Like the famous fighting bulls, the lineage of these animals traces back to prehistory. Their presence is central to Spanish culture.

As curious as it may seem to some of you, pigs and hams reflect an idealized set of Spanish values, much as cowboys rounding up longhorn steer are idealized images of America's past. The free-range ibérico pigs capture a romantic view that the Spanish people treasure: the simple valor of the frontier, a nation with a calling, and a sweeping land that sustained people on their mission of re-conquest.

Pigs and dehesa

As is the case with the fighting bulls, the Ibérico pigs are cared for by people who do not think of them as a commodity, but as creatures of worth. It is fascinating that Spaniards use the term "sacrificar—to sacrifice" when referring to the slaughter of their animals. For me the word connotes a closer relationship between man and animal than we normally think of in America. It means that the death of the animal has a sacred dimension in the human's daily living.

On a more recent trip to the region, Tim and I visited a cooperative of farmers, some of whom were dedicated to producing jamón ibérico, arguably the finest ham in the world, for export to America.

As we toured the facilities with our friend Abel, we realized that this was no ordinary meat-processing plant. These people view the production of their jamones as a work of art. No expense is spared in their quest to produce the best. They even record the genealogy of each purebred breeding sow and her offspring. They monitor every detail of the piglets' lives to be sure that they are treated well, with ample room to roam and enough acorns in their diet. This creates the ideal conditions to produce the coveted pata negra, a meat beautifully marbled with a rich, nutty flavor. As we talked with some of the artisan workers we could sense their pride.

Spaniards ritualize and sanctify the loss of life as no other people that I know of—whether it is in the profound processions of Semana Santa, the ritual in the bull ring, or the traditional late autumn matanza, where the whole town gathers to slaughter (sacrifice) their animals in preparation for the lean winter months ahead.

Hams are omnipresent throughout the land. Black bulls may appear more heroic, but ham from the pigs is more immediate. You will see plates of sliced jamón everywhere. During the Christmas season, whole hams hang by the hundreds from grocery store rafters. During the year you will find that every café proudly displays a ham on a stand (with several more to back it up).

When I read that Columbus included Ibérico pigs among his "passengers" as he sat sail on his second voyage of discovery, it underscored the importance of the Ibérico pig to Spain. He intended for them to multiply in the New World and thereby nourish the valiant Spanish settlers for years to come.

The parallels to the American romance with the Wild West are fascinating. Spaniards repopulated the land by granting land for families to herd sheep and tend their Ibérico pigs, much as Americans populated the expanding western frontier by establishing homesteads for sheepherders and cattle ranchers. When Spaniards savor wafer thin slices of their jamón ibérico, it evokes images of the forests and the shifting frontier—much as we in America romanticize a big sizzling steak that we prepare with pride on our outdoor grills.

The more I travel the byways of Spain and meet her generous people, the clearer it becomes to me the affinity Americans and Spaniards have for one another. The incidents of history cause us to appear to be different, especially since America is such a young country. But we share the core values of valor, an independent spirit and the interdependence of family.

Happy pig

The Sherry Sisters

This is a tale of three sister cities about sixty miles south of Seville: El Puerto de Santa María, Jerez de la Frontera and Sanlúcar de Barrameda. Two centuries ago several families in these towns promoted sherry wine, and their offspring continue to produce it.

Sherry's distinctive odor wafts out of the windows of centuries-old bodegas that line the streets of each town. I fondly remember the familiar aroma saturating the air when I lived in El Puerto with my young family. We would wend our way through her narrow cobblestone streets to reach our home on Calle Larga. Warehouses stacked high with American oak barrels filled with aging wine flanked the adjoining streets.

Sometimes we would step out of our house in the old part of the city and head down the block to a depósito—a small shop located in the corner of the Osborne bodega. There, for pennies, we could decant all the sherry we wanted into whatever container we brought. We usually took along an old La Casera bottle, or (heaven forbid) a glass liter Coke bottle.

Just last week I found that the custom remains. Ruth and I visited the boutique bodega Gutiérrez—Colosía and our new friend Juan Carlos dispensed for us a liter of his fine manzanilla wine in an anonymous plastic bottle!

Several El Puerto families have been involved with sherry for generations. As you can tell by their Scots and Irish names, such as Terry, some sherry families intermarried with people from the British Isles generations ago—for it was the United Kingdom that first discovered and then embraced the sherry culture.

British raiders who invaded the port of Cádiz centuries ago traveled a few miles inland to Jerez and discovered the remarkable wine made from

Bodega Gutiérrez-Colosía, El Puerto de Santa María (Cádiz)

palomino grapes. The news spread to England and the new sherry wine was enthusiastically embraced.

The surname of a leading El Puerto family was Osborne (originally a Scottish name now pronounced oz-born-ay). If you have travelled the byways of Spain you undoubtedly have seen the giant black silhouette of an Osborne bull looming on the horizon. Originally a "Veterano" (type of brandy) label was emblazoned on the bull's side, but when a law was passed to outlaw outdoor billboard advertising, they merely painted out the words. What you see now when you drive by the eighty-odd bull signs throughout Spain is viewed as a folk national monument.

Sherry is the normal white wine for the native of southern Spain. In fact, it is the bestselling white wine in Spain. It is consumed as an aperitif with tapas, served with meals, mixed with La Casera or Sprite to make a wine cooler and is the beverage of choice at major ferias. One year I visited a fair in the hilltop town of Arcos de la Frontera, where it seemed that everyone, young and old, was consuming bottles of fino and manzanilla sherry as if they were Coke!

This scenario may sound incongruous to some of you, because the first and only exposure to sherry for many Americans was in their grandmother's parlor. With graciousness, she served sweet cream sherry from her crystal decanter. It was a sign of gentility and hospitality—an English convention from another era. Sherry was hardly what it is now in Spain, a crisp refreshing wine served with tapas. It is a fun-loving drink for all.

Down the road from El Puerto is the seigniorial town of Jerez de la Frontera. The Frontera (frontier) referred to was the line between Muslims and Christians—breached in the thirteenth century when knights from northern Spain re-conquered the city. Some of their descendents have resided in Jerez for centuries, and own several of the fine sherry bodegas in the city!

Jerez has a charm all its own, with plazas lined with orange trees and the rich aroma of sherry bodegas wafting through the evening air. I might add that there is another aroma wafting as you approach stables of the celebrated Real Escuela Andaluza del Arte Ecuestrea, home of the Pura Raza Española (Andaluces) horses, and what are known as the Lipizzaners.

Perhaps the finest time to visit this delightful region is late April and early May. Jerez celebrates a meaningful Semana Santa with processions that are more for the townspeople than tourists. The world-renowned processions are held in Sevilla, just an hour away.

Jerez is also noted for vineyards that produce sherry and artisan-aged vinegar. Continuity is maintained using the solera aging system. Wines of identical types are kept in groups of casks stacked in ascending grades. The "blender" draws off wine from the oldest stock, replacing it with a similar amount of wine from the second oldest cask and so on, so that the wine moves on progressively.

One of my favorite events in Spain is the Feria de Caballo (Horse Fair) that occurs annually during the first week of May. Along with aficionados of authentic flamenco and bullfighting, horse lovers gather from around the world. Beautiful horses carry handsome caballeros and lovely señoritas in traditional costume as classic carriages drawn by magnificent teams of horses pass by in parade.

The third sherry sister, Sanlúcar de Barrameda, is a classic coastal town of Andalucía that is pretty much the way it was twenty years ago. It is a short drive along the Atlantic coast from Cádiz to its site at the mouth of the Guadalquivir River, which used to be navigable all the way to Sevilla. Columbus drew the crew for one of his voyages from the local men of Sanlúcar.

Across the mouth of the river is El Coto de Doñana, Europe's largest nature preserve for migratory birds. You can visit it by taking a tour on a small boat. Each spring during Pentecost hundreds of thousands of gypsies and other pilgrims cross the estuary on their way to honor Nuestra Señora del Rocío.

Next to the piers several remarkable restaurants feature the freshest of fresh seafood, direct from fishing boats. Sanlúcar is famous for a rare local langostino, a large shrimp/lobster, which is harvested by hand. I have treated myself to a cazuela of langostinos al ajillo—similar to gambas al ajillo (garlic shrimp) but with a richer flavor. It certainly was worth the price.

When you head to town from the waterfront and its long wide beaches (where they hold horse races each August), you will stroll along a broad tile promenade lined with palm trees. Along the way, you will pass one of the bodegas that produce manzanilla, the celebrated light dry sherry made only in Sanlúcar. The air is laden with its aroma.

Manzanilla is the driest and most delicate of all fortified wines, with exceptional fragrance. It is a light, pungent white table wine with just enough body to match the flavors of seafood and the enormous range of tapas for which Andalucía is so famous.

I am indebted to Javier Hidalgo, of the Bodega La Gitana, who provided much of the information about manzanilla. His cousin Juan Hidalgo is a good friend of ours and members of my family have visited the La Gitana bodega on several occasions.

I learned that Sanlucar's unique microclimate allows the palomino grapes to be aged under a thick layer of living organisms known as flor. The insulation provided by flor forms a natural barrier between the wine and air, producing a light white wine very low in acidity because any vestiges of oxygen dissolved in the wine must are absorbed by the flor.

The conditions necessary for the growth of flor require the bodegas to be oriented toward the sea in a north-south direction so they will receive the sea breezes that help keep humidity consistently high. A barrel made of American oak is the best container in which to age manzanilla and all sherries. The older the barrel is, the better. In Sanlúcar, many of the barrels in current use have been there since the bodegas were founded.

Within seconds of being poured, manzanilla's fresh and natural bouquet fills the air. Javier Hidalgo reported that in the late nineteenth and early twentieth centuries, the whole town of Sevilla smelled of manzanilla in the early morning hours, for this was the time of day when wine from Sanlúcar was delivered to local taverns and grocery shops. Wine loaded onto boats in Sanlúcar was transported along the river Guadalquivir on the evening tide. On arrival at the port of Sevilla, the large barrels known as bocoyes were loaded onto carts drawn by horses or mules for distribution around the city.

What distinguishes manzanilla from its close cousin fino (produced in Jerez and El Puerto de Santa María), is the microclimate, unique to Sanlúcar. The same grapes, harvested at the same time and transported a few miles to Jerez de la Frontera produce the dry crisp wine called fino, which is not quite as light in flavor. That is because the inland city of Jerez is not tempered by Atlantic ocean breezes.

The next time you travel to southern Spain, be sure to visit the sherry sisters and their bodegas. You can enjoy the langostinos and August horse races on the beach in Sanlúcar, the portside seafood cafes in El Puerto, or the horse fair and fine restaurants in Jerez. All of them are enhanced by the taste of manzanilla and fino.

Supporting Local Artisans in Spain

Every time Ruth and I visit Spain, we look forward to visiting friends we have made over the past years, many of them families whose products we bring to your table via our family company, La Tienda. They certainly are friends, not merely vendors. Whatever business we do with them is confirmed with nothing more than a handshake, often while enjoying a generous meal.

Our family takes pleasure in introducing fine Spanish food to people across North America, but we get our greatest satisfaction in supporting artisan producers who faithfully retain the tradition of excellence and pride in what they are making.

We enjoy visiting them at their place of work. Artisan is a word that is often bandied about in advertising copy, but what I am referring to is the real thing: food made by individuals, and often by hand.

We look forward to enjoying a glass of sherry and a plate of langostinos with Miguel and María Valdespino, and like to drop by to see Santiago and Raúl in La Alberca where they are curing our fine Ibérico hams. In Priego de Córdoba, we visit with Fermín and his family who press our most popular olive oil.

We particularly enjoy sitting down with Lola. She and her friends work together to produce income in their tiny village of Villarubia, which was devastated when the only factory closed and put their men out of work. They make homemade gazpacho, and two Córdoba classics: ajo blanco, an olive oil and almond soup, and salmorejo, a thick, soothing variation of gazpacho where the flavor of the tomatoes is moderated by the inclusion of bread.

We encourage many others as they preserve their traditional ways. Our friend Esther toasts and glazes her tempting almonds just as her grandmother

Pepitu at home making fresh gamaneo cheese, Cangas de Onís (Asturias)

taught her as a young girl. In Oviedo, Carlos continues to make extraordinary Mallorquina cookies in the bakery his grandfather founded in 1929. He uses lots of fresh heavy cream, and each cookie is hand dipped in molten dark chocolate before being packaged to be on their way to tables in America.

José lives on the banks of the Rías de Arousa y Muros in Galicia, where his family harvests tiny clams just outside his home. In the morning, José, along with his son and daughter, "cherry pick" the very finest sweet, tasty ber-berechos. After meticulously preparing them, members of José's family place each little cockle in a tin to form a tiny spiral. When you open the tin in your home, you will see a work of art, not a commercial product. They have been doing this for generations.

Perhaps the most satisfying story concerns the family of María Ángeles and Juan Antonio and their daughter Paloma, whom Ruth and I met in their farming village in La Mancha. Their family produces what a leading gourmet critic in Spain proclaims as "the most exquisite saffron in the world."

Once a year in the fall, they go out at dawn with their neighbors to harvest crocus flowers, sort them and toast the stamens by holding a silk mesh screen over a fire. Theirs is a long-standing family tradition.

A few years ago, sub-standard saffron was smuggled into Spain from Iran, and nearly destroyed the market for the precious saffron from La Mancha. The illegal saffron may be inferior in terms of the depth of color and pungency of flavor, but it is cheap—and most of us in the supermarket would not know the difference until we started using it while preparing paella, or any other dish dependent upon its pungent flavor and deep color.

Many in the town of Minaya lost hope. Family after family ceased growing their crocuses. Out of necessity, some had to plow up their small fields for a more profitable crop, and their children moved to the city. The tradition was dying. It is a familiar story in the world of artisan food production.

Preparing preserves in village of Malpica de Tajo (Toledo)

Tino making chocolates, Gijón, (Cantabria)

Our family thought about what we could do to help—not only to guarantee the finest quality of saffron for your kitchen in America, but also to preserve a tradition that stretched back to Moorish times. Our decision was to consolidate all of our orders for premium saffron from La Mancha and place them with María and José.

Not only were they delighted that they could continue to make a livelihood the traditional way, but the order was large enough that they convinced some of their neighbors to return to their roots and begin to grow crocuses again. In a small and unsung way, La Tienda made a difference.

The world is a better place when we care for one another, and honor each other's labor. Many of you experience that satisfaction when you patronize your local farmer's market. Not only is the product better, but also you know the person who grew it. We are extending this same philosophy, as best we can, to support our neighbors in Spain who keep the tradition alive with their hands. I hope you enjoy more of their stories in this section.

Saffron Farmer:
He Learned to Walk Behind a Plow

As we drove across the flat plateau of central Spain called La Mancha, Ruth and I were going to meet one of the last artisan saffron families in Spain. It was an urgent mission for La Tienda. We are committed to support as many quality artisan producers as we can.

Saffron has always been one of the world's most precious products. It is the hand-toasted stamen of the crocus flower—a flower similar to those you see every spring in your garden. It has been cultivated since ancient times in the Near East. The Moors brought with them the condiment *az-zafaran* (saffron) during their occupation of Spain over a thousand years ago, and until recently, over 70% of the world's production was grown on the high Castilian plateau known as La Mancha.

As in our country, shifting trade agreements and industrialization can push traditional craftsmanship to extinction. The town of Minaya, the goal of our journey, is a dramatic example. Thirty years ago, the population of the town was 3,000. Since then, two-thirds of the population has left, and those who remain include many people in their eighties.

Minaya is a typical small city of Castile. As we drove into town we saw a plaza mayor enclosed by low buildings of similar design. A venerable old church stood firmly in one corner, and across the plaza we could hear the voices of children in a school that was bustling with activity. We drove slowly through the silent, sun drenched side-streets of this farm community. White stucco buildings and elusive street numbers flanked the roads. Then we saw the friendly face of María Ángeles Serrano hailing us from the green door of her home.

Saffron producers María Ángeles Serrano and Juan Antonio Ortiz

She greeted us warmly, introduced us to her husband, Juan Antonio Ortiz, and shepherded us through her modest home, across a small patio and into her workroom. It is there that she weighs and prepares her family's precious crop. The shelf on the wall displayed examples of the small handmade ceramic urns that hold some of the finest saffron she sells. María ordered them months ahead of time for delivery to La Tienda, since each one is hand painted and fired in a small artisan kiln.

We launched into an animated conversation about the process of preparing the harvested flowers. Once they are picked (what a back-breaking job!), they are spread on a large table located in the old municipal market. Thirty or forty older ladies pick through the flowers with skilfull speed. They pick the stamen from deep in the flower, retaining the entire stem including its lighter-colored ends. This proves to the buyer that this is authentic saffron and not an imitation.

As with any precious product, the production of saffron leaves room for unscrupulous practices, such as adding foreign substances. This subterfuge is more easily accomplished with saffron called coupé—where the stamen is picked further from its base—eliminating the less flavorful light yellow ends. The uniform color of the coupe stamen makes it easy to dilute the selection with such substances as cheap, dyed corn silk.

Since Middle Eastern saffron is flooding the market, quality is a matter of survival, as well as pride, for María Ángeles and her family. On each bottle they affix a seal that says D.O. La Mancha. It is a quality control designation awarded by an independent association that guarantees the authenticity of the famous saffron grown in La Mancha.

María's husband, Juan Antonio, joined in the conversation as he described the next step in the process. The stamens are placed in a poplar sieve-like container called a cedazo, with a screen of silk. They are then toasted over a very low fire. Originally, the toasting was done over charcoal, but now a gas flame is used. Juan remarked that he liked to toast his saffron longer than his wife, making a drier product. Their young daughter, Paloma, joined us. Her dad remarked that she followed the tradition of her mother. They all agreed that they could tell who had done the toasting by tasting a saffron thread!

Finally, María Ángeles brought out an ancient woven basket filled to the brim with intensely bright and fragrant saffron. She proudly said that their daughter and son David shared their love of this ancient product. This was welcome news to us, for it assured that the tradition would continue for another generation. It was especially meaningful to Juan Antonio and María Ángeles because theirs is the last remaining family in Minaya who knows how to produce exquisite saffron.

Artisan quality saffron is not just a matter of putting bulbs in the ground. This tradition has been passed on from father to son, mother to daughter for over one thousand years. The particular microclimate of this village is recognized as producing some of the finest saffron in the world. It is a product that absorbs all the strength and intensity that the land has to give.

As Juan Antonio reached in his pocket and spread a few crocus bulbs on the table, we learned that the harsh winters and blistering summers of Minaya are perfect for the bulbs. The climate minimizes the danger of fungus and mold that would destroy them. Every year or two, the bulbs are split and rotated to keep them healthy.

Neighbor ladies removing stamens from fresh crocus flowers

The flowers are harvested in late October when the bright harvest moon shines on the emerging blooms. By dawn there is a dramatic carpet of purple as far as the eye can see. Aided by their neighbors, the Ortiz Serrano family gathers the flowers as quickly as possible before the blooms close for the day. They repeat the process for several days until all blossoms in the field have been gathered.

Juan Antonio is a dignified man who loves the land he has tilled for so many years. He carries within him the knowledge of many generations. What I appreciated most was that he was a true traditionalist. He told me he prefers plowing with a mule, even though most of the time he uses a tractor. Sometimes for recreation, he goes plowing with a bunch of the guys in town and their mules. Juan Antonio reflected "I first learned to walk behind a plow."

Minaya, long ago

After being guests of Juan and María Ángeles for a sumptuous meal at the local truck stop, Ruth and I left town with a deep sense of satisfaction. There is something very reaffirming when you spend a few hours with people of the soil.

¡Viva Lola!
The Sauce That Saved a Town

I would like to tell you the story of some remarkable women Ruth and I met one spring. Our hearts were warmed by being with people for whom adversity became an opportunity to do something better. Through their vision and hard work, these women assisted working mothers, preserved a precious social tradition, and made available to all of us the artistry of their cooking.

Our story begins when a sugar beet refinery was built in rural Córdoba during the early 1950s. Parts of Spain faced famine, and Andalucía was barely awakening from the economic devastation wrought by the Spanish Civil War and the isolation caused by World War II. The factory, Azucarera San Rafael, was a boon to the region, as they processed locally grown beets into sugar. Before the factory was founded, only subsistence farming provided income to that part of rural Córdoba.

Shortly after the factory was constructed, the village of Villarrubia began to take shape. Workers built their houses close to the factory and a nearby school so it would be easier to return home for the mid-day meal and siesta. This desire to integrate all phases of daily life: work, school, food preparation and dining, is the basis of traditional Spanish culture. Inter-related families work together and support one another for the good of all. In the small town of Villarrubia, families were able to sustain the natural rhythms of their lives.

Every day the family would arise, children would head for school, father would go off to the Azucarera, and mother would go to market for fresh produce. The rest of her morning was spent preparing the mid-day meal for her family, who would gather from work or classroom at about 1300 or 1400 to share the central meal. After they enjoyed their meal together, family

Lola León Gallego

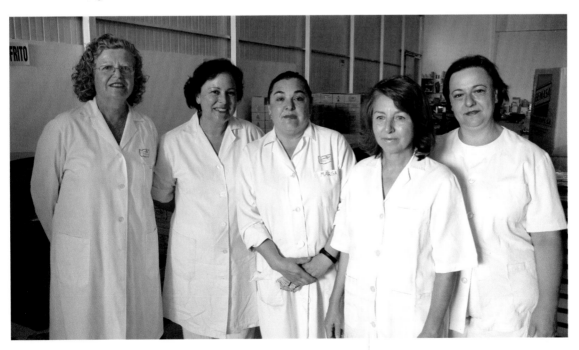

Lola León Gallego, Amalia Moreno Conejo, Margarita Almagro Calderón, Paqui
Hermoso Palomino and Ana Sierra Rosales

members would relax or nap, and then head off to school or work until they would rejoin at the day's end.

But then a shattering event occurred: after over forty years of production, Azucarera San Rafael closed its doors. The owners could not sustain any more losses and had determined that their business was no longer viable, leaving hundreds of people without jobs. The traditional fabric of life became frayed.

Fathers no longer could go to work and come home to be with their families at dinnertime. Many of them travelled over the countryside—some as far as the city of Córdoba (about an hour away), looking for any job to bring food to the table. Many mothers had to leave the home too, in search of income. If the family was fortunate enough to gather for the mid-day meal, it had to be something made quickly, for there was no one home during the morning to prepare the traditional fare that had been integral to their daily experience together.

When Lola León heard the news of the plant closing, she recognized the pending crisis. There was no time to be lost. She gathered with some of the other mothers at the local center in Villarrubia, and inspired them to take action to protect their way of life.

For years, Lola had dreamed of creating a selection of traditional products that would make it easier for working mothers to continue the tradition of serving good food to their families. She thought of her treasured recipe for sofrito, the cooking base for almost every Mediterranean meal. The mild pepper and tomato sauce would be especially valued by working mothers who had pride in their own cooking, but did not have time to maintain the quality demanded of traditional recipes. Many other women responded enthusiastically, suggesting recipes from their mothers and grandmothers—all typical of the traditional cuisine of Córdoba province.

They rolled up their sleeves and worked to make Despensa la Nuestra (Our Pantry) a reality. For the next year the women gathered and tested recipes from home, took classes to learn the standards required for food preparation, and planned the layout of the kitchen where they would work together. There were labels to design, food resources to identify, equipment to buy—the details seemed endless. Nevertheless, through diligence Lola's dream became a reality. Today the combined labor of many families produces some of the finest artisan food in Spain.

Over ten years later, the original group of women still works at Despensa la Nuestra. In addition to Lola, who is the mother of Lola and Melissa, there is Amalia Moreno, a mother of two daughters, Gema and Sandra. Her husband is Manuel, a builder. Margarita Almagro is married to Matías, a farmer, and they have two sons, Matías and Sergio. Ana María Sierra and her husband José Antonio have two daughters, Ana Belén and Lola, who go to school in Villarrubia with the rest of the children. Paqui Hermoso lives at home with her dad, since her mother died. In their rural town, these women have created an amazing commercial kitchen, which produces the highest quality artisan foods for our tables here in America.

Lola and her friends believe in what they are doing. Theirs is a vocation, not just a job. The mothers on the staff come to work before dawn so that they will finish in time to pick up their children at the village school. The children come home from school as they always have, and Mom continues to serve her family a wholesome, traditional mid-day meal. Women without young children finish the daily cleanup at the commercial kitchen, so that their "sisters" can go home. It takes some sacrifice on every one's part, but there is never a complaint.

When Ruth and I visited Villarrubia, Lola greeted us with a warm and expansive smile. With great pride, she introduced us to the women who were hard at work in a spotless kitchen. One was stirring a caldron of fresh crema de coliflor (cream of cauliflower) soup. Another was bottling some tomate frito. In the storeroom, we saw nothing but the highest quality ingredients. They were even using organic Señorío de Vizcántar extra virgin olive oil—the very favorite olive oil of the Tienda community and the one that we use in our salads and sauces at home.

We sat at a long table where Ángela, who spoke perfect English (which she learned from her Swedish boyfriend!), and Lola proudly served us their products—all of them were probably better than anything we serve from our kitchen at home! As I remarked before, it warmed our hearts to be with people for whom adversity became an opportunity to do something better. Other people share our enthusiasm. These dedicated women have received many national honors. Such fine, down-to-earth people are doing the best they can to make their world a better place. Hats off to Lola and the women of Villarrubia!

Pepe Ruiz:
Maestro of Paella Rice

A man of the Murcia countryside, Pepe has strong rustic features, dancing eyes and a jovial smile. Should you attend any of the major food expositions in Spain, you will probably see him with a glass of wine in one hand and a spatula in the other, as he presides over four paellas simmering simultaneously at the booth of his cooperative of Calasparra rice growers. That is, if there is not a traffic jam in front of his stand.

Before you know it, he will catch your eye and invite you in. Donning a simple apron, made of the same cloth used to bag the cooperative's rice, he will move to the rear where he will scoop out a portion of homemade paella and serve you with an infectious smile. His favorite is a family recipe made with snails and rabbit. During any one fair, around 5,000 people will enjoy paella made by this unassuming paella maestro!

Pepe is happily married and a proud father of two young daughters, ages five and nine. He was born and raised in Calasparra—the home of his father and two grandfathers. Pepe was handpicking rice at the family plot even before he reached school age! When as a young married man he became a rice grower himself, he followed in the footsteps of many generations of his family. Currently, he leads an association of 160 rice-growers.

To the casual visitor, the town of Calasparra may seem like any other agricultural town—akin to one you might see in the American heartland. It is located in rural Murcia in the southeast part of Spain and consists of a few essential stores: one for hardware and farm necessities, a pharmacy, a small food store and a gasoline station with a modest restaurant adjacent to it. Ruth and I visited there several years ago and enjoyed a delicious "down-home" meal. We ate amidst several local families who made us feel at home.

Pepe Ruiz with his famous paella

You can buy rice at gas stations in Calasparra

Calasparra is not merely another farm town, however. For thousands of years the area has hosted many cultures, beginning with Neolithic people from the Stone Age and Argars from the Bronze Age. Since 1412 Iberians, Romans, Moors and Christians have lived there. That was when the Prior of the Crusader Order of San Juan de Jerusalén granted Calasparra the privilege of settling fifty farmers along the riverside.

It is in Calasparra that rice growers cultivate the most celebrated paella rice in Spain. With all the lowland rice paddies that dot the eastern Mediterranean shores, you may wonder how a remote, inland mountain town ever got into the business of growing rice. A few centuries ago, a malaria-like epidemic became rampant in the renowned Algarve rice fields in Valencia. The number of deaths was devastating, and in the interest of public health the government decreed that rice cultivation would have to be relocated outside heavily populated areas.

While searching for a remote rural setting suitable for farming, some rice-growing families happened upon an exquisite microclimate a few miles from the thirteenth-century monastery of Caravaca de la Cruz. The area is 1500 feet above sea level, with readily available water flowing from the Sierra del Puerto Mountains.

Over the years, the rice growers restored an abandoned Roman aqueduct to feed water from clear mountain streams into the fields below. At first they followed the traditional four-phase cycle of preparing the land that has been done from time immemorial: sowing the seeds, weeding, and harvesting. To solve the health problem associated with standing water, they diverted the life-giving mountain streams to flow over a series of descending, enclosed terraces before returning to the main stream. This was quite a departure from the standing water of the Algarve rice fields.

An unanticipated consequence was that the rice took much longer to mature, making the grains of rice exceptionally dehydrated. This was perfect for absorbing the high amounts of rich broth needed to make great paella. Today the Cooperative of Virgin de la Esperanza is one of two sources for this unique paella rice—highly valued for the amount of broth it can absorb without becoming creamy or sticky. With the help of the cooperative's director José "Pepe" Ruiz, La Tienda is able to package our Peregrino brand bomba and calasparra rice—a precious grain unique to one tiny area of the world.

And so we come full circle to Pepe. Rice growers are his neighbors and friends. He appreciates the trust the growers have placed in his leadership and is committed to serving them. He is a man of integrity: he enjoys who he is, and what he and his neighbors contribute to the cuisine of Spain.

Paella:
The Signature Dish of Spain

Explore with me one of Spain's signature dishes, paella. In many parts of Spain, this famous rice dish has been a tradition for centuries. Some communities even have paella festivals with giant pans that serve two thousand people at a time!

Creating delicious paella is well within the reach of a regular cook. If you use authentic ingredients to start with, you do not need to be a master chef to prepare something delightful for your friends and family. I know you will have fun experimenting. It can even be a common project, with everyone pitching in to prepare a perfect feast.

Ruth and I appreciated the versatility of paella when we had to plan the rehearsal dinner party for our son Jonathan and his bride Stacey a few years ago. We were to hold the party in a rented house in North Carolina's Outer Banks. Rather than struggling with the logistics needed to stage a sit-down dinner in a strange town, we decided to serve festive pans of paella graced with local seafood.

We were no experts—we just thumbed through Penélope Casas' *¡Paella!* cookbook and selected appealing recipes. I assembled the key ingredients, including fresh seafood from the local fishing boats. Then Ruth cooked seven paellas of various configurations—some with seafood, many without. It was great fun, and it was a big hit with the wedding party, contributing to the celebratory atmosphere.

Where does the name "paella" come from? Some say the dish was first prepared by a lover for his fiancée and that the word is a corruption of para ella (meaning "for her"). Others say that paella is from the Arabic word

A feast!

Paella party

"Baqiyah," which means "leftovers" (which were tossed onto the rice). More likely, though, paella takes its name from the two-handled cooking pan, paella (from the Latin patella, meaning pan), in which the dish is traditionally made. Paella originated in the eighth century, when the Moors first brought to El Palmer, Valencia, sacks of a strange white grain called rice. Local Valencians garnished the rice with readily available ingredients—vegetables, snails, and perhaps a rabbit—and the original paella was born. It was everyday food for field workers, not a gourmet item garnished with shellfish and other seafood.

Due to the prevalence of marsh malaria in the Albufera wetlands, Valencians ceased growing any rice there from 1448 until 1860. They believed that the rice was a carrier of the disease! As I mentioned in the preceding essay, this is why our friends in Calasparra started growing rice in mountain valleys high above sea level, far away from the disease-ridden marshlands.

It was not until 428 years later that locals were convinced that it was not the rice, but the mosquitoes in the flatlands that bred malaria. From this moment on, the Albufera rice fields flourished. It is also from this time that outdoor cooking of paella became popular as a festive family event in Valencia. No longer was it simple workers' fare.

As tourists from other parts of Spain vacationed on the coast in the summer, the dish spread throughout other regions. Variations have evolved to include locally available produce. In Sevilla and Cádiz, they add big prawns and langostinos. Along the Costa del Sol, mussels, prawns, ñora peppers and lemons became favored ingredients.

Remember, paella is a simple rice dish. So keep it simple. Use Spanish short-grained rice, such as bomba. It absorbs prodigious amounts of broth, with each grain remaining distinct. Arborio rice is creamy, Asian short grain is sticky, aromatic basmati rice is fragile, and regular long grain is not absorbent. Use real Spanish saffron. In poorer times, Spaniards substituted "colorante," a yellow artificial coloring, but it is not the same thing. Finally, pay attention to your broth, it is the key ingredient. Make a flavorful broth for the rice with fish, chicken stock or in a pinch, bouillon cubes.

Paella can come in handy at the most unexpected times. In the aftermath of Hurricane Isabel, we were without electricity for days on end in Williamsburg, Virginia. Undaunted, one of our neighbors set up his paellero (propane burner and tripod). With a paella pan and whatever ingredients were at hand, he put together a delicious paella to feed the whole neighborhood!

A perfect recipe? Probably not. But for me the authenticity of paella is gauged by the community it builds. What better way to enjoy your friends than to sit around the communal paella and share it together? That is what life is all about.

José and Amalia Salcedo, founders of El Navarrico

José and Amalia:
The Soul of a Nation

If you wish to experience the soul of a nation, the source of its values, you must visit its agricultural heartland and meet the people whose lives are intimately tied to the cycles of nature.

The heart of a nation, whether in Spain or the United States, is beyond the stimulating excitement and innovation of the city. Cultural monuments, such as castles or the Statue of Liberty help you glimpse what the country values. However the statue or castle is not the country. Its fundamental nature is reflected in the people, the setting in which they live, and the fruit of their labor.

You can experience the essence of the national character when you look into the face of María Ángeles from La Mancha, who continues the tradition of her saffron-producing family while she waits for the few days in the year when crocuses bloom (see "Saffron Farmer: He Learned to Walk Behind a Plow"). Then there are the dancing eyes of Jorge, a native of Andalucía who travels the countryside encouraging small family bodegas to share their traditional wines with America ("Jorge Ordóñez: A Shepherd of Wine"). Or the weathered face of Jesús, one of generations of fishermen from Galicia as he reminisces about his boyhood when he learned to harvest berberechos (cockles) at his grandfather's side.

To get to know these people has been my family's privilege over the years as we traveled the byways of Spain to meet the small family suppliers who provide their products to La Tienda—and ultimately to your table. Other than the rare privilege of being able to work side by side with my family each day, the greatest personal satisfaction I have received from La Tienda is the opportunity to meet Spaniards who are "the salt of the earth."

I would like to take you with us to Navarra, an ancient kingdom in northern Spain. The goal of our journey was to visit the Salcedo family. They have built a growing business, El Navarrico, from the rolling fertile countryside that surrounds the agricultural town of San Adrián. En route, we stopped in Olite, a medieval village we first visited in the late 1960s. With many fond memories rekindled, we spent the night at the Parador (Spanish inn) created from the summer castle of a fourteenth-century king of Navarra.

The next day we took a country road from Olite to San Andrián and stopped by an octagonal church in Eunate, alone in a vast field. It was built by the Crusader Knights Templar who were inspired by the architecture of Jerusalem. A few minutes later, we stopped to walk down the cobblestone streets of Puente la Reina where thousands of pilgrims have passed on the way to Santiago de Compostela. As we entered the city, we revisited the wayside church known as El Crucifijo, a favorite place of mine due to the poignant crucifix carved by a pious German pilgrim.

However, I digress. Important as cultural sites may be in understanding the character of Spain, our goal was to meet the Salcedo farming family, to see what they had accomplished with their labor.

The approach to the bustling agricultural town of San Adrián, where the Salcedo family live, is quietly dramatic. Maybe I am an incurable romantic from the city, but the sight of rolling hills, one after another, with a variety of crops growing in the rich soil is very affirming.

José and Amalia started their enterprise very modestly in the 1960s. In their farmhouse they bottled whole peaches for their own use (peaches are a prized product of Navarra)—along with fruit preserves, and a variety of peppers. They shared this bounty with friends in the village.

Their neighbors told them how extraordinary their preserves tasted and urged them to make the product available in the market. One successful product led to another: hand-tended white asparagus, artichokes, alubia beans, and of course the wonderful piquillo peppers which are unique to the region. Before they knew it, they had a prospering business and brought in their children to help.

As we drove into the parking lot at El Navarrico we were greeted by Patxi, grandson of the founders. He extended the hospitality of his family to his new friends. The air was pungent with the aroma of piquillo peppers, the pride of the Lodosa region of Navarra. It was the right season to visit. Truckloads of the luminescent rich red peppers, fresh from the fields, were tumbling out of the small trucks into waiting bins. Workmen sorted them on the spot. Some went directly for roasting; others were stored for a few days so they could ripen further. Piquillo peppers are distinctively shaped, with the modified triangular form of a small trowel or shovel, hence their name.

Patxi led us into the food preparation area. We saw the fresh peppers traveling on a conveyor belt through an ingenious machine that removed their core and seeds and then flash roasted them. Next, we saw a line of local women who prepared the peppers for packing. They picked them over, removing any seared or burnt outer skin. We learned that the discarded skins were delivered to local ranches where they were served as treats for their fighting bulls.

After this meticulous preparation, the peppers were ready to be bottled in their own juice. No additives or chemicals were used. A young man at the end of the production line checked each bottle to make sure that the cover was secure. These same bottles are on our shelves. It is as simple as that; not much different from what José and Amalia did in their home.

As we watched the process, the bell rang—a signal to the help that they could leave their stations for their two-hour lunch. (No burger at the workstation for them!) Patxi invited Ruth and me to join him for a meal. As he escorted us to his car, he proudly showed us the rest of the warehouse, which was stacked to the ceiling with beautifully-packed vegetables and fruit—the cream of the crop.

We exchanged stories about our families as we enjoyed platefuls of delicious local foods such as menestra soup, astonishingly buttery alubias beans, guindillas, guernica and piquillo peppers. Patxi spoke admiringly of his uncle Pepe, the only son of the founders, and how together they carry on the heritage that Patxi's grandparents, José and Amalia, had painstakingly established.

We left with a feeling of satisfaction. It was fascinating to see how the people and the fruit of fields came together in their native setting. More than that, we found it reassuring to have met a member of the Salcedo family. His pride in the common labor of his family was abundantly evident. In 2010 this family is marking its fiftieth year of working together in the deep fertile valleys of Navarra. It reflects the soul of Spain.

Jorge Ordóñez

Jorge Ordóñez:
Shepherd of Wine

As I look back over the past decade and more, I find that one of my greatest satisfactions is the personal relationships I have formed with the people in Spain with whom we work. Almost without exception, the bonds my family and I have formed with each of them reaffirm my respect and love for traditional Spanish culture. I may wax rhapsodic about the beauty of this venerable culture, but be assured it is based on the fact of our daily contact with colleagues in Spain.

I would like you to meet my friend Jorge Ordóñez, whose creative energy is exceeded only by his generosity and warmth. I first heard of Jorge when we were reconfiguring our wine presentation at La Tienda. He suggested a couple dozen high-quality, high-value wines, and we were very pleased with his selections.

In summer 2004, Jorge learned that Ruth and I were going to be at Fenway Park to celebrate our fortieth wedding anniversary at a Red Sox game (an inspired present from our sons). When he is not in Spain, Jorge lives in greater Boston with his wife and two young children. So he invited us to join his family and close friends for a Fourth of July cookout.

When we arrived Jorge greeted us with a warm abrazo and a delighted smile as he ushered us into his kitchen, which was filled with the delicious aromas of Spanish cooking. He was in the midst of preparing fish as he would in his home in Málaga.

His wife Kathy introduced us to her mother and friends who were seated in the back yard at a long table overlooking the Charles River. Amidst lively conversation we enjoyed corn on the cob, Spanish delicacies, wedges of watermelon, superb wine and the company of their delightful young children Mónica and Victor, along with a fine young man who had just graduated from high school. I cannot think of having a more enjoyable Fourth of July.

Jorge is from Málaga, along the Mediterranean coast of southern Spain. He grew up working in his family wine distribution business, loading trucks, visiting wineries and learning first hand all there is to know about the wine business. When he went to the University of Córdoba he met his future wife Kathy, who was spending her junior year abroad in Spain. Their courtship spread over four years. Eventually they married and settled in the Boston area where Kathy grew up.

Of course, part of his heart was always in his beloved Spain. Armed with his considerable knowledge of the wine-making tradition and his understanding of the taste of Americans, Jorge set out to visit the small family wineries he most respected. He sought to encourage them to be pioneers in introducing the wonderful wines of Spain to his adopted country. When he began, Spanish wines were essentially unknown in America. Now, through partnership with artisan vintners, these wines are recognized as among the best in the world. Many earn scores in the nineties from wine connoisseur Robert Parker.

This did not happen overnight. It was the fruit of Jorge's tireless dedication and unbounded energy. What became the Jorge Ordóñez Collection was not purely a matter of selecting the best wines with which he was familiar. He improved his selection by earning the trust of traditional wine-making families and assisting them as they adjusted to modern taste—the wines themselves as well as their commercial presentation.

There is a lot that goes into the bottle of wine you have on your table. In October of that same year Ruth and I, two novices, visited one of the wineries Jorge recommended in the small town of Haro in La Rioja Alta. The Muga bodega was founded seventy-five years ago, and the family tradition has continued through the founder's sons, Isaac and Manuel.

Their accommodating assistant, Jesús Viguera, showed us how they make their oak barrels on site and told us of the process of rotating the vintage from one barrel to the next. He also explained that they consider the shape and weight of the bottle, and even the quality of cork.

The Muga family obtains their corks from a Portuguese family they have known for years. Some of their corks come from the bark on the branches of the cork tree; other corks are made from the bark of the trunk. Each source has its own qualities. The best are very dense, and exclude most outside atmospheric influences. To my astonishment, I learned that corks for the best Muga wines may cost as much as one euro each!

When we finished our tour we were ushered into the tasting room to sample four or five typical wines. Soon we were served a freshly prepared platter of huevos revuelltos con chorizo (scrambled eggs and chorizo sausage) and were warmly greeted by Manu Muga, one of the sons and owners.

Jesús spoke of Jorge Ordóñez with great respect. He said that Jorge was a man who expected their respected winery to meet the highest of standards. His visit is a serious event for which they prepare with great care. Each time he visits they find in him a warm and gracious partner who has as much respect for them as they do for him.

During a typical visit, Jorge and one or two associates taste wine from many casks. They take careful notes about the subtle characteristics of the wine in each barrel. Finally, they blend the wine. For example, for one wine Jorge may select forty-five percent of the juice from tempranillo grapes in barrel sixteen, another twenty percent tempranillo from barrel twenty-six; ten and five percent respectively from mazuelo grapes in casks two and eight; ten percent from the gracielo grapes in barrel two. He blends them with the nose of a true oenophile. Finally he might adjust the blend by adding a touch of tempranillo from yet another barrel. The result: a new vintage of a particular wine is born.

This indefatigable and unassuming man visits many bodegas in the course of each winter and spring. His goal is to promote the unique virtues of wine from the country that he loves, as well as to offer the many fine wines of his personal collection. Jorge impressed upon me that the future of Spanish wine production lies in the grapes native to Spain, produced by artisans, and appreciated for their special qualities—not in high volume products.

What I find most appealing about Jorge is his integrity, his lack of pretension, and his joyful approach to life. When he recommends wines to La Tienda he does not list costly bottles of wine that might bring him more income. Instead, he includes wines from across the spectrum that are good values for their price. He wants you to enjoy life through the wines of Spain. And I must say, I find joy in his company.

The Men of Jumilla, Miguel Gil and his brother Angel

The Remarkable Men of Jumilla

Last spring Ruth and I met three men who produce wonderful products near the remote mountain town of Jumilla, located in a coastal mountain range in northern Murcia. The mountains are about 90 km from the Mediterranean port of Alicante.

As we approached the area, we saw the haunting image of gnarled and blackened grape vines dotting the hillsides, each of them struggling to find life-giving water. Every day the vines face adversity due to the extremes of the arid mountain climate. The grapes bake in the summer sun and hunker down for the cold nights. Yet under the stony surface of the vineyards, their roots draw moisture from shallow chalky soil on a bed of limestone that absorbs the scarce rainfall.

Many of these plants have lived for nearly eighty years in this harsh environment. Dedicated vintners tend the vines by hand throughout the year. The grapes remain on the vine until they have reached their absolute ripeness, and then they are gathered and sorted by hand before they are pressed. They are the source of remarkable wines.

Miguel was the first man we met. He graciously invited us to join him, his wife Marisu and their young son Miguel for lunch, featuring the best rice dish in the world. We drove to a modest restaurant named Paco Gandía in an inconsequential town, one of those unpretentious places that only food lovers know about.

There, in a small room overflowing with delighted Spaniards, we were served "the best rice in the world." It was made with rabbit and fresh local snails simmered in a bed of Calasparra rice, saffron and spices. As I looked into the open kitchen, I could see a stone hearth fuelled by dried clippings from the vineyard. Over the crackling flames our delicious fare simmered in a paella pan. It seemed to be a cross between paella and arroz a banda. It was the best.

Later Ruth and I walked the land with Miguel. We saw those valiant gnarled vines and visited his family bodegas; both were a balance between tradition and artful technology. They produce extraordinary wines such as Clio and Juan Gil.

During our walk, Miguel stopped by a container filled with items that had been cleared from his father Juan's office years ago: the first electric typewriter in town, elaborate American short wave radios etc.—signs of an imaginative and progressive man. However, before he could reach his prime Juan suffered an untimely death, leaving his grieving wife to raise their nine children.

With heroism and determination, she nurtured a very close family through the aftermath of the horrifying Civil War, followed by the hunger and deprivations of World War II and beyond. A tribute to her strength and character as a mother is that even now her sons and their families maintain intimate ties with one another. The younger brothers work side by side to produce some of the most noteworthy wine in the region. The sons named their bodega Hijos de Juan Gil after their beloved father. He would have been so proud.

The second person we met was José María Roch, another man of great integrity. As we stood outside his centuries-old finca, he pointed out his various vineyards, planted on the hills in such a way as to take advantage of the micro-climate. José María cultivates his family's vineyard, Julia Roch e Hijos, traditionally and naturally. He uses no irrigation and minimal chemical products.

He spoke to me fondly of the venerable vines that were growing at our feet, and showed us the family's traditional bodega. At dinner, José María told me that when as a youth he chose to work with the land, his brothers questioned his judgment. They chose technical careers in the modern economy. Now, he said with a sense of pride, they appreciate his wisdom—for through his labor the family is producing Casa Castillo, an internationally-celebrated wine.

Juan Molina was the third man of Jumilla with whom we spent time. He is the fifth generation to operate a ranch called Casa Pareja. He does not produce wine, but rather olive oil and fruit. Juan drove us throughout his 800-acre holdings. A nursing field dog decided to join our excursion (with her puppies tagging along) as we drove slowly by groves of organically raised olive trees nurtured from olive pits. Ruth and I marveled at the way row upon row of old olive trees seemed to be prospering even though their trunks arose from a bed of stone! Some of the trees were ancient—surely older than any of the grape vines.

We stopped at a cluster of small buildings where Juan proudly showed us his grandfather's olive press situated within the patio. He fondly recalled that as a little boy he would be at his grandfather's side, watching as the olives arrived from the groves and then were pressed the traditional way. A mulch of the ripe fruit was sandwiched between discs of woven esparto grass and pressed until the olive oil flowed.

Juan ushered us through a formidable oak door that he had rescued from an abandoned monastery. In the corner of the next room sat a magnificent desk, entirely hand carved and fitted from olive wood. It was at that desk where he, his father, and his father's father transacted the family enterprise.

Juan is completely committed to the concept of traditional natural farming in all aspects, even though Jumilla has an inhospitable climate. He has even found a way to mix his olive pits with manure in order to produce fuel!

Juan's approach to cultivating the soil is not easy. In fact, life has been difficult for him and his family. Nevertheless, he is convinced that it is the right thing to do. He was an organic farmer before the term became fashionable. I sensed the pride he felt in his life's work as he asked Ruth and me to sample his freshly-pressed olive oil.

Vineyard at Jumilla (Murcia)

After two extraordinary days, we left Jumilla with a deep appreciation of our hosts. The fruit of their labor—the gnarled vines and olive trees and the treasured products they produced—were the result of resilience, determination, and grace—all qualities that create these remarkable men of Jumilla.

Hans & Daida de Roos, Can Solivera

Hans and Daida: Artisans of the Olive

The fragrant aroma of rosemary and lavender filled the air as I unwrapped a small treasure that had just arrived from Spain. It was a bar of olive oil soap made by the hands of Hans and Daida de Roos following a medieval recipe. They prepared it within the walls of their finca (country estate) whose foundations were laid in 1034.

What makes the soap even more remarkable is that it is made exclusively of 100% extra-virgin olive oil from Hans and Daida's own grove of arbequina olive trees. Soap of this quality, made of olive oil rather than tallow, is what made "castile" soap the gold standard in Europe for centuries. Today most olive oil soap contains only a small percentage of olive oil, and it is probably of "lampante" quality—meaning it is unfit for human consumption.

Hans and Daida are a fascinating couple. I was introduced to them by a La Tienda patron, who told me of their exquisite arbequina olive oil made in a medieval finca north of Barcelona. That piqued my imagination. Since Ruth and I were headed for the Alimentaria, the historic Spanish Food Fair in Barcelona, I emailed Hans and Daida to see if we could meet.

They responded by inviting Ruth and me to be their houseguests, sight unseen! Hans dropped by our hotel on the last day of the Alimentaria and drove us north along the Costa Brava to their home near La Bisbal. Hans ushered us into their home, named Can Solivera, where his wife Daida met us with a smile. She had recently come in from the olive groves that she had been tending with some local people from the village.

Who was this generous and expansive couple, and what was their Spanish connection? Over the first couple of days, and now a few years, Ruth and I have come to know them quite well. They have visited us in Virginia, and we have traveled together, visiting Sos del Rey and San Juan de la Peña in the Pyrenees. They have become a significant part of our lives.

Daida's grandfather, Paco Minguell, came from a small village close to Arbeca, the origin of the arbequina olive tree. During the roaring twenties he opened the first and only shipyard in Barcelona. As a shipwright he built sailing ships out of wood, equipped with a small steam engine. In conjunction with his shipbuilding, Paco also operated a sawmill. But he found that the best ash wood necessary for strong masts was in scarce supply. It seems that most of the ash trees in Spain were felled to build the ships of the Spanish Armada back in the fifteenth century. (Isn't it amazing how one act can have such an impact on our environment?)

Undaunted, Daida's grandfather went to Finland—a land of mighty forests. In addition to finding beautiful ash trees, he fell in love with a beautiful blonde. It was love at first sight and soon they were married. The newlyweds returned to Spain to live.

Their daughter (Daida's mother) eventually met a young Dutch doctor who was touring Spain on a bicycle. Soon they married and moved to a small village near Rotterdam. During the most violent days of the Spanish Civil War, Daida's grandparents sought refuge in the Netherlands. Coincidentally, Daida's mother and Hans's mother lived in the same village and became good friends before Hans and Daida met.

Hans, as you can gather by his name, is pure Dutch. His father was the pastor of the church in Delftshaven, Holland. This was the same church where the pilgrims sought refuge from English persecution in the 1600s. While part of this congregation, the refugees made plans to sail for America where they founded the Massachusetts Bay Colony near Plymouth Rock.

Hans, the bright and industrious pastor's son, earned a full scholarship to Nijenrode—the finest business school in the Netherlands. There he met and married Daida, who became a close companion through all of his adventures. The couple lived in various parts of South America for twenty years, where Hans fashioned a successful career in chemical distribution through the sea-lanes.

Advancement within the company called Hans back to Europe. In 1975, while they were stationed in Madrid, Francisco Franco died. Across the nation there was great anxiety as to the country's political fate. Hans and Daida had great faith in the Spanish people and invested in the emerging Spain. They bought property in Catalunya, Daida's ancestral home.

Hans and Daida restored their home, Can Solivera, with the same loving attention that they invest in everything they do. When they bought the building with the intent of restoring it, they found that many additions were built upon the original foundation. Most of the additions were built in 1068; the latest was 1624. They wanted to preserve as much of the flavor of the building as possible.

Hans and Daida retained the original kitchen with a walk-in fireplace and a bread oven imbedded in the wall. They preserved the twelfth-century wine kitchen that had a modified funnel for a floor so that during harvest a huge number of grapes could be stowed there. The juice dripping through a hole in the sloping floor used to be gathered in casks in order to ferment into wine.

Hans and Daida treasure Spanish olive oil. When they settled into their new estate they planted a grove of arbequina olive trees and personally nurtured their growth. Through their own toil and the blessing of a favorable microclimate, they now produce a sublime extra virgin olive oil. They literally pour the fruit of their labor into bottles.

Hans needed a miller who would be willing to take on the labor-intensive task of pressing his first small harvest of arbequina olives. Antonio was the young man he found. He was operating his own medieval-style olive press situated next to groves of wild olive trees. As Hans's production grew he was able to find a cost-effective mill closer to home.

However as a separate venture, Hans urged his new friend Antonio to harvest the organic wild olives he found around him, and press them using the modified medieval methods he had developed. Hans bottles his remarkable wild olive oil. (See "One of the Last Medieval Olive Oil Mills.")

As you can see, no grass grows under Hans's feet. In the process of conducting olive culture research, Hans discovered a medieval recipe for making soap in the olive oil museum of Baena near Córdoba. He and Daida wanted to see if it was possible to replicate this pure, healthy product and turned part of their home into a laboratory. The result is the cake of soap I held in my hand. Daida continues to make their soap, cutting and wrapping each bar by hand.

What a fascinating story involving medieval Spain, Catalunya, the forests of Finland, the ports of Holland, South America, and even Plymouth Rock! It all traces back to Spain and the ingenuity of a warm and generous couple who love working in her soil.

One of the Last Medieval Olive Oil Mills

Once upon a time, a man named Antonio Rey was born in a hamlet located along the Ebro River in Zaragoza. I suppose it was not a particularly noteworthy event, yet there are people whose lives are quietly remarkable—even though the self-important world may not take much notice.

Antonio had an engineer's heart. From the time he was a boy he enjoyed taking things apart and putting them together. If he had access to even rudimentary tools, he was happy employing his innate gift to repair whatever needed attention.

When Antonio grew to be a young man, his family helped him purchase a gasoline station. In addition to filling people's gas tanks he made minor auto repairs. He married and bought an older home in town that he looked forward to renovating. With his wife, María Cinta, Antonio settled down to what they anticipated would be an uneventful but fulfilling life raising two boys, Pau (now eighteen) and Joseph (now eight).

However Antonio's life changed forever on the day he rummaged around the basement of his new home and found parts of an antique olive mill— of the kind used for centuries before the advent of electricity. He became enthralled by this relic of another era. Antonio spent days tinkering with the inner workings of the machine, studying its construction, and tracing its history. Pumping gas and making auto repairs was one thing, but his heart was with the olive mill.

It was not long before he wanted to spend his life replicating the antique tradition of olive pressing, using the same processes that his ancestors had

76

Millstones, antique olive press, Mequinenza (Zaragoza)

employed hundreds of years before. Olive oil production has always been central to the life of the people of Tarragona, but the noise of the whirring blades and spinning centrifuges of modern production have replaced the simplicity of an earlier time. To follow his quest, Antonio needed to find an olive mill in working order, as well as the accompanying press. He searched all over Spain, and finally, in far-away Córdoba, Antonio located a classic olive mill. It was said to be one of the oldest operating mills in Spain before it had been "put out to pasture."

Hans de Roos, Antonio Rey, Don Harris and Jonathan Harris

The question was where to locate. The mill needed to be near his home so that he could still support his family. Yet it should be near the olive trees where he could feed his soul.

An impressive hydroelectric project was underway not too far from his town. It involved building a dam at the confluence of the Cinca and Ebro rivers. The project entailed flooding a valley and relocating the village called Mequinenza high above the waters of the new dam.

When the mountain village was relocated, they discovered hundreds of wild olive trees that had not been tended for years. It was the perfect spot for Antonio to realize his dream of building an authentic medieval olive mill. The olive groves surrounding the site were the epitome of organic farming since they had grown naturally for centuries.

Olive trees grown in lower altitudes are devastated by a white fruit fly that can only be combated by spraying the branches with insecticide. Wild trees grow at a higher altitude, where prevalent winds keep away the pest. There is no need to disturb the ecological balance with pesticides.

My son Jonathan and I caught up with Antonio at his mill near the wild trees. Our dear friends, Hans and Daida, who are deeply involved in the culture of olive oil, introduced him to us. (You can read more about Hans and Daida in the previous essay.) One sunny April afternoon, Antonio ushered us inside his unassuming building to see his pride and joy: a fabulous antique olive mill composed of three conical granite grinding stones weighing more than two tons each. They rotated on a horizontal millstone that weighed another 5,000 pounds.

Local farmers provide Antonio's mill with olives gathered by hand from neglected groves—some with 200- to-300-year-old trees. Because the trees are wild, not cultivated, the blend of olives varies with each harvest.

Farmers bring in small tractor loads of olives. The olives are then blown with a fan to remove twigs and leaves, washed, and fed into the area of the mill where the massive granite cones converge. Here they are crushed into a paste composed of up to sixty percent water derived from the olives and twenty-five percent olive oil. The remaining fifteen percent is fiber and pulp from the pits (huesos or "bones" in Spanish). In modern mills, stainless steel blades whirring at over 1,000 revolutions a minute produce this mulch.

The proud man then escorted us over to the press itself, where he showed us the labor-intensive job ahead of him once the paste is produced. Antonio has an upright steel spindle upon which he mounts filtering discs, about three feet in diameter, with a central hole.

For centuries, these discs were made of esparto grass, tough as palm fronds. In one of his few concessions to modernity, Antonio uses polypropylene discs that are easy to clean and do not become rancid with oil. In addition, they impart no flavor (as esparto grass does) so the purity of the oil is not affected.

Patiently Antonio stacked the discs one by one, manually spreading about a two-finger depth of crushed olives between them until he created a seventy or eighty-layer sandwich. Then he pressed out the oil with a hydraulic press driven by water.

This is what "first cold press" originally meant: olives mashed and then pressed. Today the phrase is an anachronism. A centrifuge accomplishes Antonio's laborious process in the twinkling of an eye. "Pressing" is a thing of the past.

The next stage was the most fascinating for Jonathan and me. Rather than purifying the fresh oil through a second centrifuge followed by commercial sand and filters, Antonio follows a tradition that stretches back to Roman times. He decants the oil—using nothing but gravity.

The fluid streams into a series of masonry cisterns, which have three levels of steps. In the first cistern eight inches of oil float over twenty inches of water and impurities. The water, which is heavier than the oil, drains away, and the purer oil flows to the next cistern where the process is repeated. The same thing occurs in a third cistern. By now water and impurities have been left behind and pure golden oil is deposited in large underground masonry cisterns that keep it at a constant cool temperature, protected from the light.

It takes a man of dedication and conviction to preserve the traditional way. Antonio's is a life of hard work and sacrifice to achieve his dream.

What is the difference between wild olive oil pressed the medieval way and oil extracted with modern technology? Antonio would point out that there are some olive flavors retained only in his oil, since the traditional method of oil extraction is not as efficient as the centrifuge. Also his oil has more texture (syrupy) and still tastes great long after centrifuge oil has gone stale.

But much of the difference is intangible. With a great deal of inner satisfaction Antonio knows that the fruit of his labor is close to the earth. He uses no filters and no machinery. The result is pure olive juice from wild trees derived the way it has been for thousands of years.

Antonio's mill is one of less than a half dozen olive mills in Spain that preserve the medieval way. What does the future hold? His son Pau, age eighteen, works at his father's side when he is not at school. He shares his father's pride in this remarkable labor. On the other hand, Pau told Hans the other day that he also is intrigued by IT—information technology!

The Rodríguez Family: Fermín, Aixa and Sofía

The Taproot of Spain:
Priego de Córdoba

I find it fascinating how our roots draw nourishment from many sources, and often result in something quite beautiful. As an analogy, I think of our favorite Señorío de Vizcántar extra-virgin olive oil, which contains the oil from three distinct strains of olives. It lacks the pristine flavor of a single-fruit olive oil such as arbequina or picual, but has a rich complexity that is very satisfying.

Thousand-year old olive tree of Fermín Rodríguez in Priego de Córdoba

What goes for olive oil applies to cities as well. While growing up in Boston, I could see how a culture with strong English roots was changing; Sicilian immigrants populated the North End and "Southie" was the turf of Irishmen. Yet somehow it has all worked out and the city is richer.

You might think that mine is an American story, but it is all of our stories. In Spain, for example, as you walk through the old Jewish section of Córdoba you come face to face with a timeless structure—a huge cathedral enclosed by a classic mosque that was built over a fifth-century Visigoth church!

The town where Señorío de Vizcántar is produced is Priego de Córdoba, a jewel set among the dozens of sparkling white cities that dot the countryside of Andalucía. It is situated strategically on the crest of a small mountain, with a commanding view of olive groves that stretch as far as the eye can see. In medieval times, Priego de Córdoba was the center of a thriving silk trade nestled in the rugged terrain between the Mediterranean port of Málaga and Córdoba, then the magnificent capital of Islamic Spain.

When you visit Priego de Córdoba today, you can still see remnants of this time of great wealth within the narrow cobblestone streets of the Arab Quarter, the handsome civil architecture and the stately residences. Its large, baroque marble fountain still draws from a subterranean spring, a source of water since Carthaginian times.

Ruth and I first visited Priego de Córdoba in 2001, searching for an olive oil that would serve as the signature olive oil for LaTienda—a personal selection made by our family to grace our tables at home. Fermín Rodríguez invited us there. He is a gentle man whom we had met at the Alimentaria, a giant food fair in Barcelona.

During our time with Fermín we visited a formal room where the local olive oil was evaluated. Fermín is one of the professional tasters who determine which of the freshly pressed oils from that region are worthy of the designation D.O. Priego de Córdoba. He and his fellow tasters pour several oils into small cobalt-blue glass cups, colored so that the taster is not distracted by the color of the oil—which has nothing to do with its quality. Each cup is covered with a clear circle of glass to capture the oil's aroma.

The tasting process is the same as for fine wine—after all, both wine and extra-virgin olive oil are juices; they are just from different fruit. A taster selects a cup and cradles it in his hand to warm the oil—somewhat as you would a brandy snifter. He breathes in the fragrant aroma, and then sips the oil, savoring its freshly-pressed complexity. Since the extra-virgin olive oil of the Priego de Córdoba D.O. is a blend—not a single-fruit olive oil—accurate evaluation of the balance of flavors is critical.

Just as there are a variety of grapes that produce distinctive wines: cabernet, tempranillo, or garnacha, different olives such as arbequina, hojiblanca and picual yield distinctive extra-virgin olive oils. Some have the clarity of a single variety. Some are a blend. Which is best is a matter of taste.

We kept in contact with Fermín over the years. When eight years later we heard that he was married and a father, we decided it was time to make a special effort to visit our friend. It was a daunting task to climb the mountain and navigate the winding streets of Priego de Córdoba in our rental car, but the moment we made renewed contact with Fermín it was as if we had never left. There he was, now a happy family man, with a warm and vivacious wife, Aixa (pronounced eye-sha), and their radiant three-year old daughter Sofía.

He invited us to his olive groves—a natural request since olives are his life, as they were for his father, and so on for generations past. With his wife Aixa and some friends we visited his acreage near the neighboring hamlet where he was raised, and where his brothers still live. He showed us trees bearing picudo, picual, and hojiblanca olives, growing side by side, as some of them have done for centuries. We saw an olive tree that was more than a thousand years old, within whose hollow Fermín used to hide as a young boy.

I felt something almost mystical standing among the olive groves. These gnarled trees with their deep taproots are strong and timeless. I thought to myself, "I may well have been standing in a grove that a Visigoth farmer harvested fourteen hundred years ago!" And then, "The hollow that Fermín hid in as a child might have harbored another little boy eight hundred years before—much the same, except he probably would have been a Moor."

I was returning to my fascination with how our roots often draw from many sources and may result in something quite beautiful, such as Fermín's olive oil. The next afternoon, as I walked beside Aixa along the cobblestone street of the Moorish quarter of Priego de Córdoba she turned to me and laughingly said that she embodied the history of Spain. She was a Jewish Muslim Berber from Morocco with a Christian husband and daughter!

As you may recall, the Berbers crossed over from North Africa in 711 AD at the invitation of quarreling Arian and Catholic Visigoth kings. For the next 800 years an uneasy relationship existed between the Jews, Moors and Christians as they lived among one another in Spain—Al-Andalus. In 1492 the monarchy forced Jews, such as the Sephardic ancestors of Aixa's mother, to leave Spain and make their homes in North Africa. Soon the Moors were also forced to leave. They were Muslims, like Aixa's paternal family. (Unfortunately the Jews and Muslims did not get along together that well in the new setting, either.)

Aixa's father is a successful hotelier and restaurateur in Casablanca, where she and her brothers and sisters were involved in the international community in this most cosmopolitan of cities. Over the years she learned French, German, Arabic, and Spanish. She was hired as an interpreter for Fermín when he was interviewed on French television. That is what brought them together.

As they formed a new family, they became part of a continuum of olive husbandry that stretches back to antiquity. Just as his excellent Señorío de Vizcántar is the product of many different olives, so also Fermín, with his loving wife Aixa and their delightful three-year-old daughter Sofía, represent the many strains of modern Spain. It is not a perfect analogy, but I think a useful one.

Twenty-First Century Traditional

Juan and Elena Yurrita are in their mid-thirties, a happily married couple from the Basque Country who are blessed with two daughters, Nora, eight, and Irena, five (almost the same age as two of our grandchildren). They are a part of the generation that grew up in the heady years when Spain was emerging as a young democracy after the rule of Francisco Franco.

The Yurrita family has been involved in processing the famous bonito and anchovies of the Cantabrian Sea for five generations. Now the son of the next generation is building upon this rock bed of integrity by introducing twenty-first century concepts.

Juan's father, Alfonso, and Uncle Jorge are directing the family's artisan company today. It has been a family business for generations, stretching back to 1867. Originally, the men of the family were fishermen who went to sea on small boats in the Cantabrian Bay that borders San Sebastián and Zarautz.

Juan's wife, Elena, comes from a similar background. Her family has fished for many generations. Although her grandfather operated his own fishing boat, her dad broke from the mold by becoming a professional football player. From early childhood, Elena has loved to cook. She often watched her mother and grandmother making her favorite dish—delicious croquetas filled with jamón and bacalao (cod) covered with thick béchamel sauce.

Juan and Elena's parents taught them from an early age that in the food business there is no substitute for quality ingredients and careful attention to detail. For example, Elena's grandmother always made their croquetas with fresh local milk, which added an elusive richness to the final product. Juan's family business has never cut corners. They have always used only costly extra-virgin olive oil when packing their anchovies and bonito tuna.

Barquero, fishing boat

Juan explained to me that they prefer oil from the tiny arbequina olives, whose sweet fragrant flavor provides a perfect balance for the saltiness of the anchovies.

Being a fisherman has long been a time-honored vocation, and brings a certain elemental satisfaction, even though going to sea requires long hours and sometimes dangerous work. You probably know what I mean if you have ever spent any time in a fishing port, with the briny air, the hovering sea gulls and the fishermen at work maintaining their gear and repairing their boats.

The Yurrita family is a partner to these men, receiving their fresh catch and processing it with care. They support anchovy fishermen, both young and old, who go out in small boats from the shores of San Sebastián and Zarautz to gather their catch in a responsible manner. They make sure that the anchovies harvested are mature, and release the "small fry" back into the sea, so that these baby fish can grow to maturity, to be caught another day. For centuries this was the wisdom of their trade, passed from father to son, and for this reason, the local breeding stock remained replenished.

But in recent times, boats crewed by men with no sense of stewardship entered the long-established fishing grounds and almost ruined the traditional way of life of the local citizenry, by harvesting even the little anchovies—highly prized by some food fanciers. Soon the famous anchovies from the Cantabrian Sea virtually disappeared, largely because boats from outside the region used advanced sighting devices and trolling nets.

Through technology, they easily located schools of anchovies and indiscriminately harvested them, along with other creatures of the sea caught in their nets. The traditional grounds were quickly fished out. It is a familiar story—similar to what has happened elsewhere—with blue-fin tuna in the Mediterranean, codfish from the Grand Banks off Newfoundland, and oysters here in the Chesapeake Bay. Juan told me that for the last four years there have been virtually no local fish. It is only in this current season that they are regenerating, due to a total ban imposed on the fishing of anchovies.

As Juan grew up within his family business, he learned the standards of ethical fishing and careful preparation. But he noted that the recent crisis concerning the availability of anchovies from the Cantabrian Sea could happen again, and he wished to protect his family's well being by making them less dependent on the vagaries of fishing.

As a young man, even before the shortage of anchovies occurred, Juan heard of a unique food-marketing program at St. Joseph's University in Philadelphia. Specialized marketing of food was a concept new to traditional Spain.

With his father's blessing, he headed off on an educational adventure to a new land with a new language. He returned with his head full of ideas about how the family's business could prosper and expand beyond its traditional means of supporting their extended families.

Typical of the new Spanish vigor Elena, his wife to be, also left her household to earn a degree in industrial engineering. But even with their higher education, Juan and Elena had no thought of striking out on their own and leaving their families for broader horizons—as their American counterparts would likely consider doing. Both came from traditional backgrounds, and wanted to remain close to their roots; yet they prepared

Croquetas de bacalao—codfish croquettes

to meet the new demands of the twenty-first century, and the preservation of their family business.

Juan and Elena recognized several changes in Spain that could work to the benefit of their family business. Their youthful vision looked outward to new possibilities, unaffected by the national isolation experienced by their parents' generation in the aftermath of the wrenching Civil War of 1936–1939.

Quality frozen food was now available, with the infrastructure needed to maintain it. In addition, the business sector was growing rapidly and more women were entering the work force. They realized there would be increased demand for quality meals prepared for the busy professional to bring home and enjoy with minimal preparation.

In another essay ("¡Viva Lola!"), I told you of Lola and her friends who get up early in the morning to prepare traditional sauces and soups for their fellow mothers who had to work outside the home. They create a virtual pantry of handmade products so that their neighbors can maintain the tradition of sharing a mid-day dinner with their husbands and children. Juan and Elena carried this concept one step further. They decided to bring quality prepared dishes to food lovers anywhere.

When he studied in Philadelphia, Juan noticed the trend of easy-to-prepare meals becoming popular among Americans. He and Elena anticipated the demand at home. They remembered croquetas as an all-time favorite of theirs and of tapas bars throughout Spain. One food critic said that you could judge a good restaurant by the quality of croquetas served.

Four years ago the Yurrita family purchased a small building in the neighboring village of Zurnaia and developed a gourmet recipe for croquetas with the help of a local Basque chef named Andoni Eduren. They hired nine local women to make all kinds of croquetas by hand, including jamón ibérico, cod bacalao, cabrales cheese, mushroom, tuna, and piquillo pepper. Their most remarkable creation is made from chopped mussel mixed into béchamel sauce, and returned to its shell. It is sprinkled with fine crumbs before deep-fat frying. It is wonderful when served piping hot.

Juan explained to me that there is no secret to making great croquetas. As with any fine cooking, however humble the item, you do not compromise with ingredients and you make them with patience and care. Each morning a large pail of fresh milk is delivered from a friend's dairy farm. The chef mixes the milk with newly-milled flour and extra-virgin olive oil from Toledo. The fish and seafood added are the day's catch from the ocean, and the cabrales cheese comes from the neighboring caves of Asturias. Freshness is the watch-word. The ladies form the croquetas with care, just as they would in their own homes, and fry them at the proper heat. Next they are chilled, frozen and are on their way to tables in Spain and America! It is as simple as that.

One of the amazing things about the world in which we live is that through technology and commercial infrastructure, we can have on our plates in America the same piping-hot croquetas enjoyed in the homes of the Basque country. By doing so, we support families who choose not to industrialize, but rather to continue making with pride their time-honored cuisine.

La Alberca (Salamanca)

2
Continuity

El Puente del Arzobispo,(the Bridge of the Archbishop)

The Archbishop's Bridge

From the moment I set foot in Spain, I was drawn to the beauty of the Spanish people. Ruth and I traveled the back roads of rural Spain to learn how these remarkable people preserved their traditional values. We encountered villagers who were barely subsisting due to the ravages of their civil war and its aftermath. Yet they radiated a spirit that was far more precious: they cherished their children, were bonded to their families, and looked after one another as neighbors.

We came to understand that continuity is key to their way of life. It is preserved by common activities that bind the community together, whether it is fishermen in Galicia mending their nets along the shore or people working in the bodegas of a sherry town, where an omnipresent sweetness fills the air.

In Spain, the most important indication of this healthy way of life is one of the most natural: it is that neighbors and families enjoy meeting at their favorite café at the end of each day to exchange the day's concerns. The modern industrial age often severs these personal ties to the land and people. Some of you who have lived in rural America understand the quality I am referring to.

A good example is the story of Belén de la Cal Hidalgo. She and her husband, Manuel, are proud parents of two sons. Her family is the latest in a line of artisan potters that stretches back six generations. They create a distinct style of ceramics that have been produced for centuries in their village of El Puente del Arzobispo. Ruth and I enjoy eating from their cheerful plates every day.

Belén told me that her home town was founded in the fourteenth century when a key Romanesque bridge was constructed in the area. It seems that

Painter Belén de la Cal Hidalgo,
daughter

Augustín de la Cal Berreira,
Maestro Artesano

96

while surveying his lands, Archbishop Don Pedro Tenorio realized that there was no communication between two rich agricultural zones, Castilla and Extremadura, because there was no viable way to cross the Tajo River.

The river narrows where it turns toward Lisbon, creating waters that flow with great force, thereby preventing the transit of animals as well as general commerce. Don Pedro called for the construction of a bridge and commissioned the best architect of the time, who had made his reputation designing the bridge of San Martín in Toledo and the admirable Puerta del Sol in Madrid.

Work began in 1380 and lasted eight years. The granite used for the bridge was extracted from the Tajo river bed. The number of workers needed was so great that stonemasons and other laborers moved with their families from Toledo to the new village.

Belén explained that this generated a brisk trade in essential goods. The families needed tableware for daily use, containers for storing food, and ollas (cooking pots)—a necessity for every hearth. To meet this demand Mudéjar craftsmen, Muslims who remained in Christian territory after the Reconquista, settled near the bridge construction site of El Puente del Arzobispo, bringing with them the exquisite art of Moorish ceramics they had perfected in the workshops of the ancient city of Toledo.

After completing the Romanesque bridge (which still stands today) many of the workers and their families settled permanently in the area. They found they could make a livelihood due to the dramatic increase of commerce passing over the new bridge from Extremadura and Castilla.

Many took advantage of the flourishing agriculture nourished by the very rich silt washed down the River Tajo. However, the lush broom grass that grew along the edge of the water was perfect for use as fuel in potters' kilns. With prosperity, the art of ceramic crafts evolved. Artisans designed brilliant glazes with metals: copper (green) cobalt (blue), and manganese (black).

It seems as if the de la Cal family has always been dedicated to producing fine pottery for daily use. There is a 200-year record of their making tile decorations for convents and churches, as well as enamel tiles for monumental works such as the Plaza de Toros de las Ventas.

Today Belén de la Cal Hidalgo works closely with her father Agustín de la Cal Berreira, a Maestro Artesano since 1980. He has apprenticed more than 400 students, and has served as the inspiration to Belén as she learned traditional pottery-making techniques. In their studio they surround students with examples of the tradition they are committed to preserve. Apprentices learn a technique that is painstaking—requiring great patience.

Some of you may recognize echoes of Islamic art in the intricate symmetry and brilliant colors of the traditional designs. This is not surprising, since the Moors and Christians were intimately entwined as a part of Spanish culture for over 700 years, and artists from both traditions held in common many design concepts.

Belén tells me that the location of her workshop feeds her soul. It is in a natural setting, surrounded by the River Tajo, and built around an old patio. It is enveloped by echoes of the past, including an antique clay press used by people employed by her family many years ago.

Among the cottonwood trees by the river, in the company of her dogs, woodpeckers and goldfinches, Belén continues the legacy of her father and their ancestors with imagination and enthusiasm. I find it very satisfying that we are be able to enjoy her work and share it with others, in this way doing our part to strengthen the traditional Spain that we love.

Clay and Continuity

When I travel the byways of Spain I often feel an almost magical bond that connects me with the hundreds of generations who have populated this ancient land. Sometimes this is prompted by a seemingly insignificant object such as the humble cazuela: the simple terra cotta dish that has been used by families on the Iberian peninsula for thousands of years.

We can trace this type of cookware back to 1000 BC, during the time of the first Phoenicians who settled in the Atlantic port of Cádiz. As the centuries have passed, the long succession of people inhabiting the narrow Cádiz peninsula have continued to use this type of terra cotta bowl daily. Today when I visit a tapas bar in Cádiz, I am likely to be served fresh olives or a portion of sizzling hot garlic shrimp in an earthenware cazuela, not unlike those of centuries past.

The most interesting cazuelas I have encountered are from the age-old town of Breda, which is as far from Cádiz as you can travel while remaining in Spain. Nestled in the foothills of the Pyrenees north of Barcelona, Breda is close to the fascinating town of Gerona, where at various times Jews, Christians and Moors made their homes. Of course Romans lived there before all of those settlers. They discovered a rich deposit of a unique type of clay that their potters fashioned into superb cazuelas, bowls and plates.

What makes these cazuelas so special? When baked in a traditional kiln, the unique property of the clay found in this region enables it to be formed into remarkably dense and cohesive products. The Romans reinforced the intrinsic strength of the terra cotta by adding tiny pebbles before it was fired. This refractory process enabled the cazuela to have remarkable structural integrity, making it less prone to cracking. The tiny pebbles have the added

Handmade cazuela from Breda (Girona)

virtue of retaining the heat or cold of newly-cooked foods for extended periods. Today the potters of Breda make terra-cotta cazuelas from the same source of clay, following essentially the same method that the Romans initiated during the days of their legions.

When I first picked up a cazuela in Breda, I immediately recognized that this ordinary terra cotta vessel was the same shape as a Roman bowl that you and I might see in an archeological museum. In the dawn of the twenty-first century, I held an echo of antiquity in my hand. I felt that magical bond with the generations who had stood on this ground before me.

The cazuelas of Breda are not the only objects that reflect Spain's continuity. When I strolled the streets of Toledo I experienced the same connection with the generations who have walked these same cobblestones before me. As with my time in Breda and Cádiz, I experienced a magical convergence of cultures while I browsed the shops of Toledo with their Damascene style metalwork, mazapán sweets fashioned into fruit and animal shapes, and the brightly-colored plates created by modern potters who echo the symmetrical designs of Islam.

Within holy Toledo was an amazing confluence of cultures: Arian Visigoths who migrated from Northern lands, Moors who initially were Berbers invading from North Africa, indigenous Iberians, and Jews who contributed to a remarkable center of learning, where ancient texts of classical Greek learning were translated from Arabic into Castilian Spanish.

Then there is enchanting Sevilla. Toward the end of her prosperous centuries under Moorish rule, the amazing Giralda minaret was built in 1284 to complement the Great Mosque. Several years later victorious Christians transformed the Giralda into a magnificent bell tower for their vast Christian cathedral. Within the church's spacious interior lie the remains of Christopher Columbus. The stunning gold screen behind the high altar proclaims Sevilla as the crown jewel of the Christian Reconquista.

Two hundred eight years later, King Fernando and Queen Isabel designated Sevilla as the administrative hub for commerce with the New World. As I walked her cobblestone streets I was surrounded by the stately buildings that are so evocative of Sevilla's role in Spain's Golden Age.

Across the Guadalquivir River that flows through Sevilla is the neighborhood of Triana where Gypsy, Moorish and Christian cultures meld in the creations of colorful traditional wall tiles, as well as in the haunting melodies of flamenco. Ceramics abound in the hundreds of tiled entryways and patios that adorn homes and civic buildings throughout Sevilla.

Most amazing are the dazzling enamel and gold ceramic creations, replicas of those made in Moorish Sevilla's Golden Age, which came to an end eight hundred years ago. A few artisans employ the now vanishing technique of corda seca, a ceramic cloisonné glaze and gold process, to make gorgeous decorative plates.

One experiences America in quite a different way. We Americans live in a very young country, and our strength as a nation lies in our flexibility, rather than in our lineage. A steady stream of immigrants joins us, and I feel enriched by their contributions as new Americans. All of this change is invigorating, but it also can be unsettling because, unlike Spain, we do not have a long enough history in which to integrate these threads into a coherent culture.

Perhaps that is why Ruth and I, after spending twenty-six years in the Navy where we experienced many corners of America and the world, have chosen to settle near Jamestown, Virginia, the site of the oldest permanent English settlement in America. Maybe it is because we resonate with this example of continuity in America, that we so enjoy experiencing the continuity of Spain.

Beautiful tiled entryway—a home in Sevilla

La Alberca:
The Resilience of Spain

Every time I return to Spain I encounter the essence of her culture in just about every Spaniard I meet, and in every place I visit. Although recent events may have made Spain the European trendsetter, the substance of Spain remains constant. Come back with me forty years to the medieval town of La Alberca, and I will show you what I mean.

The village of La Alberca is nestled in the northern slopes of la Sierra de Francia, close to the border with Portugal. This terrain is called the dehesa, a remnant of the primeval forests that once covered Europe. It is composed of holm oak, cork oak, beech, chestnut, pines, and fruit trees, as well as meadows of wild flowers and herbs where black-hoofed Ibérico pigs have feasted upon acorns for hundreds of years—maybe even longer.

The La Alberca that Ruth and I experienced back in the 1960s was a primitive place. The roads reflected the ravages of time, and cobblestones were loose or missing in the plaza mayor with its medieval stone cross. The traditional houses surrounding the square were made of granite, stone and wooden beams. Many had three floors, each with a different function, with the bottom floor originally used as a stable for animals.

A burro or two wandered through the square while we were there, and there was a privileged pig that trotted the alleyways of the village. I learned that every year on June 13, the feast day of San Antonio, the villagers dedicate one piglet to their favorite saint, bless it, and release it into the streets to wander where it wishes.

The pig is nurtured by all until the next January. At this time it is sacrificed at the matanza, when the families in the community gather to slaughter their hogs. It requires a concerted effort to ensure a supply of meat for the coming year. At the conclusion the people celebrate their time together with a sumptuous feast in the town square.

As you can imagine, it did not take much effort for us to imagine ourselves in medieval times, hundreds of years in the past. But before we romanticized too much, we realized that the rustic touches of their local way of life were not the choice of the villagers, or for the entertainment of tourists; they were the result of poverty.

To put things in perspective, a little more than a generation earlier Spain was devastated by a horrendous civil war. It was brother against brother, father against son, and almost one third of Spain's men lay dead; in addition 35,000 priests, nuns and monks were slaughtered. The hemorrhaging nation was left to its own devices during the ensuing World War II, and for decades beyond. No other country came to its rescue. Starvation was a fact of life.

That La Alberca was a functioning town when we visited was a tribute to the resilience of the Spanish people. I found it beautifully expressed by the villagers who, despite their hard life, took time to adorn with flowers the large wooden balconies of their ancient houses.

When Ruth and I returned to La Alberca ten years later, we could see the first hints of prosperity. In the town plaza were piles of new cobblestones, with workmen artfully laying them by hand, one by one. The aura of the town was one of optimism and it was a time of rebuilding. The town had been declared a national heritage site, and tourism was beginning to bring a new face to the town.

With sons Tim and Jonathan, I returned to La Alberca in 2005. This time the beautiful mountain village was bustling with activity. We dropped off our luggage at the tasteful and commodious Hotel Doña Teresa, and drove through town to the headquarters of Embutidos y Jamones Fermín, the object of our journey.

The owner, Santiago Martín, and his family greeted us cordially and showed us their ham-curing facility, which he had sensitively designed to reflect the architecture of the town. He announced with satisfaction that they would soon receive USDA approval to export their Ibérico hams to the United States. The family exuded confidence, proud that they would be the first to bring the celebrated pata negra ham to America.

Fiesta de la Matanza, La Alberca (Salamanca) 2010

My first thought was that the Martín family members were very different from the villagers my wife and I encountered forty years before. But after
reflection, I realized that they were not so different after all. They retained the
same solid values, yet now that the economic and emotional ravages of the
civil war could be put behind them, a feeling of hope enabled them to realize their dreams. The modern ham-curing operation that my sons and I saw
before us was the fruit of dedication and years of hard work by a family whose
grandparents undoubtedly lived in the medieval town I visited in the past.

I decided to return to the old Plaza Mayor, to see what had happened to it
since my first visit. I found that the cobblestones were neatly laid out and in

good repair. The twelfth-century granite cross was still at the center. Tourists mingled with townspeople at local cafés. The houses flanking the square were beautifully restored. There were no animals sheltered on the ground floor of the dwellings.

"This is quite a change," I thought to myself. At that moment, I saw a priest with two altar boys piously making their way across the ancient plaza. One of the boys led the procession, carrying a cross. Presumably their travels would end at their parish church. As the three disappeared from sight, a mule meandered by. On his back was a bundle of golden straw. Even though it took place in the twenty-first century, the scene could have occurred hundreds of years ago.

A few years ago, one of my friends said wistfully that she was sure that the Spain she loved was no more, as we met at La Tienda's Paella and Sangría Festival in Williamsburg. We felt a common bond as we reminisced about our life among the Spanish people with flamenco music in the background and a glass of sangría in hand.

To be sure, her observation had an element of truth, just as I am not the same person I was twenty years ago, or even five years ago. All I have to do to confirm that is look in the mirror (albeit fleetingly). However, there is another truth. I am who I always have been. The essence of my personality has not changed. When I meet friends and family after years of separation, we know each other.

So it is with Spain. Much has transpired since the Civil War of 1936. Nevertheless, I continue to witness families worship and work together as they have for generations. I see in this continuity the essence of traditional Spain. I feel no regrets about the inevitable changes brought by modernity; the traditional Spain we have loved in the past is alive and well in our modern times.

Spain:
Reviving a Culinary Heritage

Spain is witnessing a culinary counter-revolution. After years of modernization, Spaniards are seeking to revive their traditional heritage. It has taken only two or three resilient generations to overcome the tragedy of the early twentieth century—the Civil War and exclusion from European recovery after WWII. What they have accomplished is an amazing turnaround.

Traditional Spanish artisans had the conviction that their handiwork was of value and would survive many lean decades. Their integrity enabled them to resist the temptations of commercialism. Now they flourish with the support of lovers of good food, in Spain and throughout the world. For example, on one trip my sons drove along the rugged seashore of Galicia to meet a couple who produce extraordinary tinned seafood. Even now, at about 3:00 AM they telephone fishermen at sea in order to anticipate and purchase the very freshest and best seafood that will arrive at dawn.

When I was on the road in rural Spain in 1965, I remember seeing a man behind a mule, his small son by his side, teaching him how to plow the land. I also saw a farmer from Galicia guiding a wooden wagon that was pulled by a team of powerful oxen. They had rabbit-fur pelts placed between their horns to protect them from the weather.

In Andalucía, I remember men buzzing off to work on their motos (motorbikes) with saddlebags woven out of esparto grass straddling the rear fender. In earlier days, they would have ridden burros. Within one of saddlebags was tucked a whitewashed terra-cotta jug (tinaja) that served as the worker's source of water as he worked in the fields. Occasionally Ruth and I would come across the painted wagons of a Gypsy caravan, with the colorfully-dressed women waving hello.

At home in El Puerto de Santa María we would go to the Buen Pastor bakery and get a loaf of handmade bread—still warm from the oven. The municipal market was overflowing with local potatoes, spinach, oranges and fresh-caught fish.

At the time, it was interesting and romantic to dip into a pre-industrial society and enjoy the way people lived centuries ago. However, for many people in Spain it was a still a time of deprivation and suffering. As I have mentioned in other essays, their modern economy was devastated by the 1936–1939 Civil War and ensuing World War II isolation—even from the Marshall Plan. To us the oxen were quaint; to them it meant they could not afford a tractor or, more to the point, rarely had a decent meal.

As people became more prosperous in the 1970s and 1980s, they replaced their oxen and mules with tractors. Workers could afford small automobiles to replace their motos. As women began to work outside the home, they enjoyed the efficiency and convenience of air-conditioned hipermercados. These supermarkets began to crowd out local farmers' markets, which are now only open in the morning.

Local bakers began putting preservatives in the dough so that the loaves they baked before dawn would stay fresh until evening when people stopped by on their way home from work. Their business declined as people bought commercial pre-sliced Bimbo, which would stay "fresh" for days. The quality of food declined because artisan items were inefficient to make. Nevertheless, the relative quality of life was better for many people.

Now their prosperity is at a point where Spaniards appreciate artisan-quality products and are willing to pay for them. Jamón ibérico used to be a delicacy restricted to the wealthy, but now the ham is available at the neighborhood tapas bar. Spaniards are able to appreciate the traditional handmade food of their past, and they are willing to support the artisans who have preserved it.

Perhaps the transportation revolution is the most amazing thing of all. Just imagine, an old woman in El Bierzo gathers mushrooms in the woods, or a shepherd brings to his village the cheeses he made in the high country of the Picos de Europa. In a matter of weeks we can enjoy their handiwork in our American homes.

Bridging Old and New Spain

Three of my most lasting images of Spain involve bridges. One is the bridge at Ciudad Rodrigo, an active rural center with a long history. It can be found in Salamanca province close to the Portuguese border.

Many years ago Ruth and I stayed in a wonderful fourteenth-century castle there—part of the national Parador system. As we stood by the open window of our room, we could see women washing clothes along the banks of the Águeda River, as their ancestors had been doing for centuries. Beyond the women was a classically proportioned bridge built by Romans more than two thousand years ago.

Puente la Reina, Camino de Santiago (Navarra)

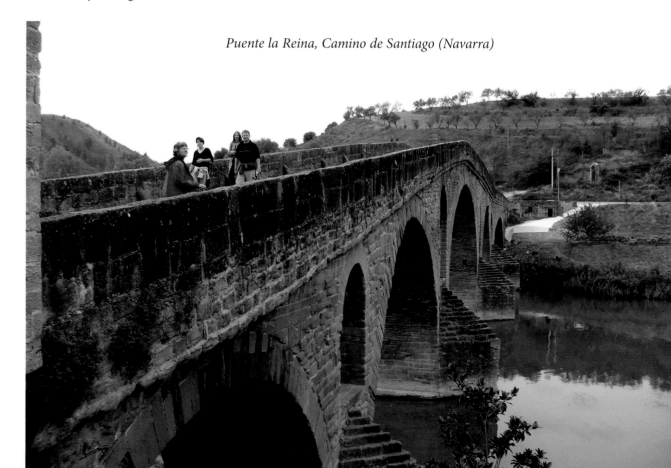

The image of the bridge, the river running through the city and the women washing clothes on the river bank could have been from any century, except when the scene was disturbed by a random truck heading over the bridge toward Portugal. Yet when we returned to Ciudad Rodrigo two years ago to enjoy a local festival, times had changed. The castle, the Roman bridge, and the vistas were there, but the women washing their clothes on the rocks by the river were not. The timeless touristic scene had been altered.

This is one of the paradoxes of being an American tourist in Spain. On the one hand we like to immerse ourselves in ages past, largely because our American culture is so new. In this case, the history of Ciudad Rodrigo dates back to dolmens in pre-history and extends to Romans, Suevians, Visigoths, Moors and Christians. On the other hand, we surely do not want to sentence the local Rodrigan housewives to hand washing clothes at the river in order to enhance our enjoyment of the past. A washing machine is a good thing!

Puente la Reina is another bridge whose image I remember vividly for its eight stine arches and its solid medieval beauty. It was built across the Arga River in Navarra by Queen Doña Mayor almost a thousand years ago to help the streams of pilgrims who were on their way to Santiago de Compostela. The graceful structure was at the juncture of two major pilgrimage routes that originated in faraway France and Holland. The town that formed in the vicinity of the bridge was named Puente de la Reina—literally the Bridge of the Queen. It is a fascinating place where you can enjoy many religious monuments contributed by the medieval pilgrims. One of the most moving is a cross in the wayside chapel "El Crucifijo," carved by a German pilgrim centuries ago.

Today the ancient streets are still crowded with travelers along the Camino de Santiago. Some are pilgrims in the old-fashioned sense: penitential Christians making their journey as a spiritual exercise, hoping to draw closer to their Lord. But you will also see hikers with no particular faith seeing the journey as a challenge, or a walk through nature. Then again, you will also see cyclists on thousand-dollar bicycles living their own personal fantasies.

So the paradox is evident once more. There is the mental image of the purity of medieval pilgrims streaming on foot across the bridge to seek solace at the shrine of Santiago. Yet, for the most part, that sort of piety belongs to another age—and who are we to question the motivation of latter-day pilgrims whose spiritual quest may be another variation of the same form? It is not as if the motivations of medieval pilgrims were pure (except in our imagination). Although externals change, the substance remains the same.

The third bridge is not Roman or medieval. It was neither built to serve the Roman legions nor the Christian pilgrims. It is one of six new bridges created to improve traffic flow for the Expo '92 World's Fair in Sevilla. El Alamillo Bridge is a dramatic cantilevered bridge that crosses the Canal de Alfonso XIII, allows access to La Cartuja, an island monastery complex, and arrives on the other shore. It links two distinct parts of the ancient city of Sevilla—spanning distinct eras.

On one side is the triumphant capitol of the Reconquista with the huge cathedral and Alcázar (built by Pedro the Cruel). On an island in the middle is an expression of Spanish monasticism embodied in the sprawling edifice of La Cartuja, home of the Carthusian monks, and later the site of ceramic tile making. On the other shore is the exotic Triana district, steeped in its Moorish past, with Moorish tile making continuing, Gypsy music and dance echoing through the narrow streets.

Out of practical necessity—the growing traffic of a newly-vibrant Spanish culture—comes this magnificent work by Spanish engineer and architect Santiago Calatrava. He conceived of a new kind of cable-stayed bridge. A single pylon inclines away from the river and supports the 600-foot span with thirteen pairs of stay cables.

Some people compare the bridge form to a harp, others to a ship's mast, still others, a swan. In this bridge I see the New Spain, innovative and daring, enhancing people's enjoyment of centuries of cultures—adding, not tearing down. The tension is always there between tradition and innovation. As Spain emerges from a long dormant period marked by suffering, I enjoy seeing her joyfully stretch her wings.

I admire Spain's legacy of art, faith and a traditional culture that strongly reinforces their commitment to family. I have to rub my eyes as I see some of my favorite images replaced, whether it is a modernized Ciudad Rodrigo, cyclists in their expensive regalia zipping across the ancient pilgrimage bridge in Puente la Reina, or international tourists sweeping into gorgeous flower-filled Sevilla. But I have confidence that Spain will digest these cultural innovations and integrate the best of them. Spanish culture remained unique, even though immersed in the Moorish culture for 700 years. I have few worries about today's Spain.

Family Leisure:
A Relaxed Approach

It is August, the height of summer, and I dream of what it would be like if my family and I were living in Spain right now. For much of the month we might be enjoying the uncrowded Atlantic beaches of the Costa de la Luz, or exploring the caves of Altamira and the new dinosaur museum with the grandkids.

Throughout Spain commercial activity winds down in August. Many firms close completely so that owners and employees can plan extended vacations with their families. Although this is inconvenient to us as importers, I appreciate the value traditional Spaniards place on leisure time with their families—an attitude toward life that extends throughout the year, not only during vacation.

When our family lived in Andalucía, the shopkeepers in our seaport town would close up in the early afternoon to enjoy a siesta, a time set aside for refreshment and rest with the family. After reopening in late afternoon for two or three hours, the shops would close for the day and the owners would retire to their favorite cafes to enjoy tapas with close friends and family members. Perhaps they would savor a caña of beer with some manchego cheese, thinly sliced jamón serrano, or a sizzling cazuela of garlic shrimp. Later in the evening some would head home to join their families for a stroll about town, known as a paseo.

On a warm summer evening it seems as if the whole town is out on the streets walking about. I find nothing more affirming than to see three generations of a family walking together: a proud young couple with a baby in the stroller, "Abuela" holding the hand of her grandchild, and all three generations in warm, pleasant conversation. This has been the traditional way of living for hundreds of years.

In modern Spain and America we find ourselves part of a culture with values that compete with tradition: convenience and individual autonomy. The slow ritual of personal interactions is thought to be "wasting time." A generation ago we depended on another person to fuel our cars. An attendant, often a local youth, would greet us, pump our gas, wipe our windshield, and check the oil. Today we can slip in our credit cards, pump our gas, and be on our way—sometimes even when the station is closed! We enjoy the same type of efficiency with ATM banking and airport check-ins. We hardly need to see a person.

Palomas y Chico, Plaza del Cabildo, Sanlúcar de Barrameda (Cádiz)

In many ways this automation is a wonderful advance. No one regrets the elimination of waiting in long lines for mundane activities, or dealing with petty bureaucrats. The new technology broadens our horizons. In an earlier time we could never have enjoyed artisan foods from Spain unless we lived near a large port. Now we can have boquerones (marinated anchovies) in Buffalo, or lomo (pork loin) in Louisville!

But if we are not careful, we can allow electronic efficiency to replace the human interactions that make the traditional Spanish way of living so healthy. I make an effort to keep two cultures in a dynamic balance so that we can draw from the best of both.

The longer our family lived in Spain, the more we learned to incorporate into our modern way of life the traditional ways of our Spanish neighbors: taking more time to be with others, thinking of a leisurely meal as a blessing, and experiencing a healthier way to spend our days and raise our children.

The long life expectancy experienced by Spaniards is a result of more than olive oil and the Mediterranean diet. It is a life where conviviality is a virtue, not a luxury. It is a traditional life where the seemingly trivial human events of everyday living—chatting at the market, dining with your family, visiting with your friends—are given the respect they deserve.

Although in both America and modern Spain we may find our automated lifestyle in conflict with the healthy way of life of our traditional friends in Spain, nevertheless it is possible to draw from the virtues of both modern and traditional cultures and be the better for it. Our family tries to live this balance every day.

Sanlúcar de Barrameda:
An Ever-Rolling Stream

It was dusk that evening in early June—about 10:00 PM. I stood on the beach in Sanlúcar de Barrameda where the Guadalquivir River merges with the Atlantic Ocean, and watched the last group of pilgrims disembarking from the barge that had brought them from the El Coto Doñana marshlands on the other side.

Sanlúcar is situated directly across from Doñana, a national park and nature preserve composed of marsh, shallow streams and sand dunes. To the consternation of the local wildlife, I am sure, it is the goal of hundreds of thousands of pilgrims. Crossing the river at that point provides the easiest access to the holy sites for those traveling across Andalucía. For centuries, countless thousands of people have forded the shallow river crossing via rafts, wooden wagons and horseback. (I can visualize quail and flamingos cowering in the underbrush!)

The group I was watching this evening were returning from the romería, or pilgrimage. They reassembled their procession and proceeded down the beach toward their homes in the village of Bonanza. A man led them, holding high a processional cross. Next, on foot, came a small group of other men who must have been the town fathers, or the leaders of the religious brotherhood devoted to the Romería del Rocío pilgrimage. They were followed by a group of men of all ages mounted on the beautiful horses Andalucía—and I mean all ages.

For me as a father, the most poignant scene was a three-year old boy who was riding confidently next to his father on his own full-size horse. His father

Villa Carmen, Bajo de Guía

leaned over in his saddle and kissed his son, so proud that his son was now a full-fledged part of the procession of young horsemen.

The procession continued with a group of men and women singing devotional songs to La Blanca Paloma, the White Virgin of El Rocío. Several walked with long silver-encrusted staffs. They preceded a wooden cart bearing a float of their local Virgin pulled by some of the stronger men, with some women on the other end pushing to help it along in the wet sand. Following them were three pairs of magnificent oxen and the remainder of the villagers.

Ruth inside Villa Carmen

They were a part of the El Rocío pilgrimage. Every year up to a million ordinary people, as well as Gypsies in colorful carts, converge on the remote town of El Rocío. They sing and dance, and flamenco songs fill the air. It all leads up to the climactic moment when the image of the Virgin, La Blanca Paloma (the Dove), emerges from the church. Some women break into tears and sing mournful saetas; others hold their infants and little children up to touch the Virgin so they may be blessed by her presence.

Then it is over for another year. The people return home by bus, cart or van, singing and visiting with one another. It is a communal event that has been going on for over a thousand years. Some anthropologists maintain that the origin of this annual gathering is pre-Christian! The liturgical rhythm of the centuries is reenacted every year, and will be for years to come. That little boy on horseback will grow into a young man, then a father, and then perhaps a leader of the brotherhood with his son by his side.

What makes the scene more remarkable is that Sanlúcar is not primarily known for the Rocío. Five hundred years ago this sleepy sherry town was the center of the expansion of the Spanish Empire to the New World! In the first five years of the sixteenth century, 300 to 400 ships set sail from this bustling port, including those of Columbus and Amerigo Vespucci.

For over 200 years, caravels bound for the Indies would cast off their moorings and head into the treacherous Atlantic from Sanlúcar. Many ships returned laden with treasure in their holds. The gold was weighed in the neighborhood of Bonanza before being sent up the river to Sevilla. Now Bonanza's glory days are over. It is just a little village—the final destination of the small group of pilgrims I saw processing down the beach.

We spent the month of June in a stately house, Villa Carmen that was built by a sherry family in the early 1900s. Its high ceilings, marble floors, tiled kitchens and patios overflowed with cascades of bougainvillea. There was even a small lemon tree against the white wall, laden with fruit, to the delight of my grandchildren.

The landlady, María, welcomed us with grace. She and her five sisters had grown up within these walls. Her husband Miguel reminisced about how he used to court her when María was a very young lady. One thing led to another and now they are a married couple of forty years or more. Miguel told us that his forebears were among the twenty-four knights who liberated the neighboring sherry town of Jerez de la Frontera from the Moors in the thirteenth century. His family has been in the area ever since.

We dropped by to see our friend Juan Hidalgo, whose family has been making sherry since 1792, when they came down from the Basque Country. Originally they were interested in refining salt, but fortunately for all of us they decided to plant vineyards of palomino grapes that now yield La Gitana manzanilla—a favorite white wine consumed at the famous spring fair in Sevilla. Juan showed us the family bodegas with their endless rows of black

American oak barrels full of the juice of the manzanilla grapes now mellowing into the celebrated wine.

It is said that when the handful of emaciated survivors of Magellan's round-the-world voyage finally returned to Sanlúcar, the first thing they asked for was a healing glass of manzanilla. Of course the story is apocryphal, since that type of wine did not exist at the time! However, we do know that the officers and men of the fleets of Lord Wellington and Napoleon depended upon the Hidalgo family to replenish their wine supplies.

When Juan showed me the office of his older brother, Luis, who now heads the company, it was if we were stepping back in time. It was the same airy, beautifully-tiled office that his father and grandfather occupied when they directed the company. Among the gallery of family members whose pictures were mounted on the wall was a portrait of their grandfather. The family resemblance was uncanny!

One final tale—and to me the most engaging. If you visit Sanlúcar in the summer, you will be surrounded by small swarms of young teenagers buzzing around on their motos (motor bikes). They seem to be everywhere, boys and girls moving together in groups. My Spanish friend explained that they are repeating the tradition of their parents who do much the same thing—going to their favorite café to visit with their same friends year after year. When these young people were much younger they were with their parents in the cafes and played together around the tables. Now they are coming of age.

I find the thought of such continuity very appealing. This stability may be what first drew me to the culture of Spain so many years ago—experiencing families whose ties go back for hundreds of years. Kids who grow up bonding with the same friends from infancy have no need to posture at the malls pretending to be what they wish they were. Their friends are life-long. They know who they are.

Except for small pockets of rural America, this is not our experience in the United States. We do not have the continuity that an age-old culture holds as a common trust. My grandparents were immigrants from Yorkshire, Ulster and Armenia. My wife's are from Holland and Friesland. Our kids have quite the combination of genes!

My family has been enriched by our immersion in different cultures and ways of life. The experience fosters a certain flexibility of worldview. On the other hand, we have not experienced what traditional Spaniards enjoy: that continuity and grounding which comes from living together for generations. As in a close family, many things are mutually understood in a society such as theirs. It encourages a sense of order.

A balance between flexibility and continuity serves us well. There is strength in this fusion of different ways of life. Had my family not come from varying backgrounds, and had we not been willing to live in many different cultures, we never would have discovered the traditions of Spain. In fact, the concept of La Tienda would never have come into being! As in many things, I am grateful for both ways of life—their blending is a wonderful thing.

Pedro Díaz

The Shoemaker's Son and the Carpenter's Daughter

When I think of St. Valentine's Day my thoughts are of Pedro Díaz and his wife Isabela Buzón, a devoted couple I met in Spain in 1975. Pedro is no longer with us; he died in 2005. But his life with beloved Isabela lives beyond him.

Pedro and Isabela embody the best of traditional Spain, and are also an example of the new Spain that has risen out of the ashes of the Civil War. Their story reflects the ensuing decades of sacrifice that gave birth to the strong and healthy Spain we know today.

Pedro the sailor at U.S. Naval Hospital, Balboa, with volunteer nurse Robin Sandford (San Diego)

Our families have formed a close bond that has grown over the past thirty years. As parents we have grown old together and enjoy each other's children and grandchildren. Ruth and I feel especially close to one of their daughters, Olga, since she lived with us in Virginia for a few months twenty years ago. Later I had the privilege of solemnizing her marriage in a medieval church in the sherry town of Jerez de la Frontera.

Pedro was the son of a shoemaker in the ancient Atlantic seaport of Cádiz, one of my favorite communities in Spain. He was born in 1934, two years before the beginning of the bitter Civil War. The 1940s and 1950s were a time of profound deprivation for the people of Spain as the shattered nation tried to piece together a cohesive life, isolated by her European neighbors.

In 1952, when Pedro was eighteen years old, he left home to join the Spanish navy, La Armada Española. Like many young men his age throughout the world, he went to sea in order to find his place in life. Providentially, he was chosen to be a member of the crew that was returning a ship to the U.S. Navy. After crossing the Atlantic to New York, the ship sailed to its new homeport in San Diego.

Pedro Díaz and his wife Isabela as newlyweds

Pedro and Isabela Díaz

In California Pedro contracted a serious lung condition, which landed him in the Balboa Naval Hospital for several months. He was alone in a strange country. His Spanish shipmates had to leave him behind because he was too ill to travel. But a warm and generous woman named Robin Sandford, a volunteer nurse, befriended Pedro. She also helped him learn English while convalescing.

Pedro was an eager learner. Student and teacher became fast friends; in many ways he became her adopted son. Recognizing what a bright and earnest young man he was, Robin gave him some money with the provision that he return to Spain and go to school once he recovered.

Pedro loved to learn. After completing school in Spain he went to Oxford for a year to perfect his English. He had no money except a small gift from Robin, and lived by his wits in order to complete his studies. Pedro maintained correspondence with his California benefactor for the rest of her life.

After his studies in England, Pedro returned to Andalucía briefly—and then left for France to learn French. This time he was totally on his own. Finally, he returned to his family in Cádiz, several years older and wiser. He intended to settle down and work with his father as a shoemaker. But he was always open to opportunities.

Pedro heard a rumor that Americans were going to establish a large naval base near the fishing village of Rota, in conjunction with the Spanish Navy. So he rode a local bus for an hour or two to Rota to meet the U.S. Navy.

The naval officers welcomed him warmly because he was one of the few Spaniards who could speak English. That day the Americans put him to work, teaching English to his countrymen. From that time on, until he retired forty years later, Pedro was at the naval base teaching Spanish sailors how to speak English and American sailors how to speak Spanish.

Rota was a little far to commute from his family in Cádiz, so he looked for a room in the neighboring town of Jerez de la Frontera. A carpenter and his family living over their shop rented a room to this ingenious young man. Soon he was included at the family table, where he came to know their daughter, Isabel Buzón. At first, she was somewhat skeptical of Pedro. He was a bit too exotic for her—he dressed with style and was not like "the boy next door." Nevertheless, Pedro had dancing brown eyes and a warm heart. They fell in love and within nine months, they were married!

The Díaz family still resides in Jerez de la Frontera, as they always have. There Pedro and Isabela raised three bright daughters: Inmaculada, Olga, and Eva. Inma is married to a Spaniard from her hometown and has a traditional Spanish family. Olga and Eva married Americans. Both sisters are teachers, following in the footsteps of their father. In fact, Olga has taken the place of Pedro in the classroom on the Naval Base. Just as her father translated letters for me in years past, now Olga translates my essays.

When I began my assignment to the Base Naval de Rota with my young family, Pedro was an invaluable partner. On the personal side he helped us get settled in the Spanish culture. He assisted me professionally by helping me locate a site for a retreat ministry I had designed called CREDO / Esperanza. You can read more about this in my essay "Don Ignacio: The Spirit of Generosity." Because of his deep faith and close ties to his church, he opened many doors for me.

Pedro opened doors for others as well. As he rose to become the intercultural affairs coordinator for the commanding officer, he worked assiduously to bring Americans and local Spaniards together so that they could work in harmony.

After years of wandering as a young man, Pedro found a spiritual anchor in his beloved Isabela who was always by his side. She is a pious woman, practicing her traditional age-old faith. With members of her ladies group at the parish, she has attended many pilgrimages, including the famous El Rocío, across the Guadalquivir River in the province of Huelva. Isabela remains a spiritual anchor today. As a mother and grandmother, she continues to lend her loving and faithful support to her extended family.

Old Spain and new: steeped in tradition, yet always eager to integrate the changing times. That is the story of the shoemaker's son and the carpenter's daughter. To my mind, people such as this devoted couple are the bedrock of Spain and an inspiration for all of us.

Miguel Valdespino and Maria Arizón

Valdespino and Arizón: 700 Years of Family History

Miguel Valdespino and his family have been around the same neighborhood for a long time. I thought living in one house for eighteen years was remarkable (and I guess it is in the United States) but when I asked Miguel how long his family had been in the area, he said it was for the last 700 years.

It seems that when King Alfonso X re-conquered Jerez de la Frontera from the Moors in 1264, Don Alonso Valdespino, Miguel's ancestor, was one of twenty-four Knights of Jerez granted land as a reward—mostly vineyards cultivated by Arabs.

It was not until 300 years later that the vineyards' fruit would become commercially viable. When the British fleet launched the Raid of Cádiz in 1596, the officers and men were delighted to taste a new type of wine from Jerez, which they tried for the first time in their forages across the countryside. The British corrupted the Spanish word "Jerez" or "Xeres" which became the English word "sherry."

In a touch of irony, sherry became the rage in Britain, developing into a profitable trade for the Spaniards. Miguel wryly commented, "The raid proved to be a good promotional campaign!" For the past four hundred years the Valdespino sherry bodegas have been the benchmark of quality in Jerez de la Frontera.

Miguel's interest spread to the neighboring manzanilla sherry town of Sanlúcar de Barrameda—not only professionally but also personally. For it was in that beautiful seaside town that he courted María, his wife of forty-five years. Her kin, the Arizón family, emigrated to Barcelona from Ireland, to escape British persecution of Roman Catholics. Miguel thinks this occurred in the 1600s—perhaps during the time of Oliver Cromwell.

Arizón is the Spanish rendition of the English name "Harrison," their surname before fleeing the British Isles. What an interesting coincidence it is that my grandfather, William Harris, emigrated from Northern Ireland to the United States in 1898! Could it be that María's family and ours are distantly related?

The Arizón family became important fleet owners, trading with America, and moved to the port of Sanlúcar de Barrameda. It was the port designated by the crown for New World trade. Columbus embarked from there in one of his earlier voyages, and treasure-laden ships returning from America would tie up in Sanlúcar de Barrameda. In the suburb of Bonanza their gold would be weighed and forwarded to the royal court in Sevilla via the Guadalquivir River. This, not the TV show, is the source of our word "bonanza"—used in the New World to refer to a discovery of dramatic wealth.

Miguel told me that in the eighteenth century one of María's ancestors became the Marqués de Arizón, a title that is still used by María's first cousin. As the Arizón family prospered, they built an architecturally-impressive warehouse complex including a manor house and beautifully decorated private chapel. The family owned these buildings for over 300 years until the government expropriated them as an historical monument.

For many generations, young Arizón men chose careers in the army, especially in the cavalry with its magnificent Andalucian horses. In the early twentieth century one of the men attained the rank of Captain General, and fought in Cuba. Even today, María's father and two brothers, including Juan, an artillery colonel, have had experience in the army.

We first got to know the Valdespinos when our family rented one of their summer places for the month of June. An old family from Sevilla built Villa Carmen in 1910 when Sanlúcar was the fashionable place to spend the summer. María's parents acquired it in 1950. Miguel reported that the handsome building "soon became the meeting place for so many of our friends and the holiday place for all the family, including ourselves when we married."

As the family expanded, Miguel bought a neighboring villa, "San Francisco." Should you visit Sanlúcar de Barrameda and drive along the shore-side avenue Bajo de Guía, you can see these majestic houses behind bowers of bougainvilleas and night-blooming jasmine.

"We married on January 10, 1963, in a double wedding," my friend Miguel related. "My lifelong friend Jaime married Mercedes (they also own part of the front of Villa Carmen) and I married María. Double weddings are rare here. We had two girls and one boy, and now have two grandsons, one of whom is studying dentistry, and the other is in his first year at the University of Navarra."

Miguel is pleased that his grandson is going to a private university with Catholic roots. He hopes this will strengthen the young man's commitment to his Spanish heritage: commitment to family, strong ethical values, and a clear understanding of right and wrong. "We all do wrong," he muses, "maybe some of us far too often. But to me the great problem is when we deprive children of the right to judge situations because all is considered normal and ("magic" word) "democratic." These are words spoken by a true aristocrat.

Each time we return to Andalucía, Ruth and I make a point to join Miguel and María at one of the many tapas bars that ring the picturesque Plaza de Cabildo in Sanlúcar de Barrameda. It is up the street from the Pedro Romero and La Gitana sherry bodegas, and around the corner from the bustling municipal where beautiful fresh vegetables and fresh seafood are brought in from the farm and ocean every day.

Miguel Valdespino and Don Harris

There, over a glass of manzanilla and a plate of tortillitas de camarones—tiny shrimp crisply fried in the slightest amount of batter—we will enjoy the companionship that is most appreciated in a relaxed and ancient culture, where time (thankfully) seems to pass us by. You might want to consider a visit sometime. There is an amazing hotel from another era awaiting you, right across the street from the bodega.

La Mezquita (La Catedral), Córdoba

3
Faded Glory

Treaty of Tordesillas, signed by Ferdinand II of Aragón
and John II of Portugal in 1494, Archivo General de Indias (Spain)

Echoes of Faded Glory

Modern Spain is complex—an amalgam of medieval kingdoms. In fact the autonomous region of Navarre still refers to itself as the "Kingdom of Navarra." When I stroll the streets of many Spanish historic towns I find it fascinating to recall the "place in the sun" they once enjoyed. It is a good way to put things into perspective, and to realize that the concerns we may think are so crucial today, are actually so ephemeral.

The city of Córdoba comes to mind. It is a pleasant regional city in Andalucía, which I visit quite often. Yet it was quite different 1,100 years ago. At that time Córdoba represented the zenith of Islamic culture, rivaling Babylon, Rome and Baghdad in magnificence and importance. Many viewed it as the greatest city on earth. At a time when few Christian monarchs could write their names, Córdoba had a library of half a million books and possessed far more wealth than all of European Christendom. Scholars and artists abounded.

A thoroughfare stretching along the bank of the Guadalquivir River was used for elaborate public processions. It had an astonishing array of shops with products from China, India, Central Asia, and the Near East. The royal market for luxury goods, al-Qayseriyya, was fabled. Taverns, caravanserais, baths, and inns served merchants and other travelers who flocked to this most important cultural center of the western Mediterranean.

Córdoba had 900 public baths and countless private baths at a time when they were a rarity in the rest of Europe. Six hundred years later there still was no effective sewage system in Europe's largest cities. Many posit that it was the influence of Córdoba's flourishing Moorish culture that gave Spanish people that unique sense of personal dignity and courtesy they still possess. This may be the best gift we have received from the glorious Moorish culture.

Today the splendor of that magnificent culture has faded. All that remains of Córdoba's glorious days is the Mezquita: the mosque now called La Catedral. Should you choose to enter one of the mosque's nineteen doors, you would find yourself in a forest of more than 860 slender columns of marble, porphyry and jasper. The columns support a timber roof, arches richly decorated with scarlet and gold. Hundreds of years ago 280 huge silver or brass chandeliers burned perfumed oil to illuminate the interior on special occasions. The largest was thirty-eight feet in circumference with 1,454 lamps. Fitted into its reflector were 36,000 plates of silver, riveted with gold and decorated with jewels.

The Mosque of Córdoba was as sacred to medieval Islam as the sublime Hagia Sofia in Constantinople was to Christendom. Is it not a monument to the folly of man that bitter religious rivals have reduced the two greatest religious structures in the West to museums? Still, when I visit them I experience some sense of the divine that inspired their builders.

Other cities of faded glory are also intriguing to visit, even though they have a less monumental aspect. One is Tordesillas, a few miles west of Valladolid, where a treaty was drawn up in 1494 that affected the New World.

It was clear after Columbus's discoveries that conflict would soon arise over land claims by Spanish and Portuguese explorers. On May 4, 1493, Pope Alexander VI took action to clear up any confusion that may have arisen. He issued a decree establishing an imaginary line running north and south through the mid-Atlantic, 100 leagues (480 km) from the Cape Verde islands. Spain would possess any unclaimed territories to the west of the line and Portugal would own any unclaimed territory to the east.

After further exploration, the Portuguese grew dissatisfied with the agreement. They realized how much more land Spain had been given. In June of 1494 the line was re-negotiated and the agreement was officially ratified during a meeting in Tordesillas. The Treaty of Tordesillas re-established the line 370 leagues (1,770 km) west of the Cape Verde Islands. There were many unanticipated, if tragic, consequences.

You may recall watching the poignant 1968 film *The Mission* with Robert DeNiro and Jeremy Irons. The movie tells the true story of eighteenth-century Spanish Jesuits who gave birth to a flourishing high culture among a remote South American Indian tribe, especially expressed by the indigenous people

The Court of Lions, The Alhambra, Granada

as they learned and performed choral and orchestral works such as Vivaldi and Corelli. However, due to the geographic adjustments proclaimed by the Treaty of Tordesillas, the Indians no longer fell under the protection of the Spaniards, and were summarily slaughtered or enslaved by Portuguese troops.

But the treaty may not be the most fascinating period in Tordesillas's past, even if it might be the most astonishing from our modern perspective. Originally a bulwark of the defensive line of the Reconquista, Tordesillas received its charter in 1262 from Alfonso X, The Wise. Eighty years later, his grandson Alfonso XI built a substantial castle with an adjoining convent.

Alfonso's son, Pedro the Cruel, embellished it in the style of the Alcázar in Sevilla. It was there that he abandoned his bride Blanca de Borbón on their wedding night, locking her up in the palace and Convent of Santa Clara in order to run off with his lover, María de Padilla. Ultimately, Pedro gave the convent and palace to his two illegitimate daughters by María.

As if that were not enough intrigue for one small town, Princess Juana, the troubled daughter of King Ferdinand and Queen Isabella became Queen of Castile in 1504, only to be overwhelmed with grief when her beloved husband Philip the Handsome died in his prime only two years later. She remained a monarch in name only, and was confined in the convent from 1509 to her death in 1555, a melancholy period of forty-six years.

Tordesillas now? It is a transit hub for trucks going from Madrid to Salamanca and beyond, with a population of 8,643 souls. Agriculture is its basic source of income. Although it is situated on the Duero, the river silted up long ago. When Ruth and I decided to visit the Convent of Santa Clara we parked our car in a broad area, almost like a playground. While young boys played soccer energetically nearby, we slipped into the convent. Remnants of the past still echoed in the chapel, not only in the elaborate ribbing of the ceiling, but also in the silent harmonium that Juana enjoyed playing as she whiled away her hours and years.

There are more wonderful cities of faded glory: Cartagena, Zamora, Oviedo, Soria, Ciudad Rodrigo, El Burgo de Osma, Sanlúcar de Barrameda—my list is long. As I said at the beginning, a way to gain a healthy perspective now is to know what has gone before. Our country is so young that it is harder to do that. But when you dig into an ancient culture such as Spain's, you learn that much of human endeavor fades. What lasts are the bonds of love we share with family and friends.

Covadonga:
Tales of War and Cheese

For a brief moment, all of Spain was focused on a deep valley in the dramatic Picos de Europa, bounded by vertical canyon walls. Like a shooting star, events in the bucolic valley of Covadonga and the village of Cangas de Onís flashed across the sky, and after a few dramatic years returned to a place where shepherds tend their flocks and make cheeses.

The fabled Battle of Covadonga was where, under the leadership of the legendary Don Pelayo, brave Asturian mountain men halted the inexorable advance of Muslim forces. Had the Asturians lost, the Christians would have been pushed into the sea, for they were located but a few miles south of the Bay of Biscay in northern Spain.

Some say it was the Virgin of Covadonga who protected Don Pelayo and his men. Others refer to the legendary account of Saint James, the brother of Jesus, who rode from the heavens on a huge white horse, flashing an impressive sword. His miraculous arrival inspired the Christian band, and for the first time, in 722 AD, Christians stopped the relentless advance of the Moorish army.

Today there is a statue of valiant Don Pelayo to the left of the basilica in Covadonga, where he seems to survey the valley of his triumph. You can visit the shrine of Our Lady of Covadonga in the grotto near the site of the battle. The earthly remains of Saint James rest farther away in Galicia, under the high altar of the cathedral in Santiago de Compostela, the goal of pilgrims for over 1,000 years.

The narrative that would be more acceptable to us skeptics is that the conquering Berber Islamic army had swept through the peninsula carving a swath of destruction. Apparently Asturian holdouts in the mountains were a cause of irritation to the Muslim leaders. The mountain defenders lured a party of Muslims (how many we do not know) into an ambush as they were traversing one of the many blind valleys of the Picos.

This was the turning point for the embattled Christians of Spain, and Covadonga became the battle cry for the Reconquista—an intermittent struggle that lasted for over 750 years and shaped the character of the Spanish people. The victorious Don Pelayo established the Kingdom of Asturias with Cangas de Onís as the capital.

About fifty years later the capital was moved to the city of Oviedo, whose cathedral possessed precious relics from the Holy Land. (You can visit the relics today in the cathedral's Cámara Santa.) Nearby in Naranco and Lillo new architecture flourished as the kingdom grew to be a major force in the reconquest of Spain. After its brief moment in the sun, Cangas de Onís slipped back into obscurity.

Even after forty-five years of traveling the byways of Spain, Ruth and I had never been to Covadonga. In early 2010 we made our pilgrimage to the site. We stayed just outside Cangas de Onís in the Monasterio de San Pedro de Villanueva. Alfonso I constructed the original building in 746 AD. Most of the current structure was a twelfth-century Benedictine monastery until it was tastefully converted into a superb Parador (rural hotel) by the Spanish government.

After we became settled, I telephoned a La Tienda friend, Jaime (Jim) Fernandez and his wife Renate. We had never met in person, yet our friendship had grown as we exchanged emails about cheese and life in Asturias. When I mentioned that we were thinking of visiting the area, Jaime graciously invited us to join them. They have owned an apartment in Cangas for the past thirty-seven years. He announced with a certain flair that he would prepare his favorite Asturian-style garlic soup for his honored visitors.

We were greeted by a warm and cordial couple who turned out to be retired cultural anthropologists, lately from the University of Chicago where Jaime still teaches the spring term, even though he is nearly eighty years old. They are no run-of-the mill academics. Both are still climbing around in the Picos de Europa, and in this way are friskier than I am (or perhaps ever was).

They ushered us into their parlor. Over glasses of fresh Asturian sidra

Grotto, Nuestra Señora de Covadonga

(hard cider) they served us two types of hand-made Gamaneu cheese—a blue cheese with a subtler flavor than the better-known Cabrales. One wedge was made in a high mountain pass (del puerto) and the other was made in the valley (del valle). Jim and Renate told us that they were putting the finishing touches on a manuscript about this rare cheese and those who make it.

I found it a joy to be with a couple who have shared life's ups and downs for years on end, and are working in harmony as companions in their later years: whether they are composing a book together, enjoying the farmers' market, or climbing in the mountains. Over Jaime's hearty garlic soup, the four of us

Statue of Don Palayo at Covadonga

traded many tales. We ranged from family stories, to other experiences we have had over the years, to our mutual love of the Spanish people.

Jaime (Jim) has strong Asturian roots. He recounted that Fernández was a typical Asturian surname, borne by his grandfather who emigrated to America in the 1870s and died at the turn of the century. After finishing school Jim chose cultural anthropology as a career because he did not want to be an academic sitting behind a desk. He taught for many years at Dartmouth, Princeton and the University of Chicago as well as in Madrid and Barcelona.

Early in his career, Jim lived with people deep in Africa, and it was on his way there that he met his future wife—by chance. Both of them were disembarking from a voyage from New York to Europe, and Jim gallantly offered to help her with her luggage. One thing led to another (another story), and he married Renate, who eventually joined him during his work in Africa.

An unanticipated turn of events caused them to settle in Jaime's ancestral land of Asturias. Life in Africa had placed the health of their very young son in jeopardy, so Jim and Renate decided it was best for the family to leave Africa. Renate found rewarding work being involved in the lives of shepherds and cheese makers in Asturias. After living in the high mountain meadows of the Picos de Europa, they moved to Cangas de Onís in the valley, so that the children could attend school.

The evening of fellowship drew to a close, but Jim and Renate were eager to have us experience market day in Cangas de Onís a few days later. As we approached the market we saw the familiar sight of a churro maker who served up a paper cone full of the piping hot fritters. Next to him a flower seller offered plenty of cheery primroses to brighten the late winter day. Nearby, a truck was loaded with the largest cache of garlic I had ever seen in one location—including rustic woven garlands that filled the truck's open gate. At the edge of the market building was a cornucopia of Spanish fruit from Andalucía: boxes full of every sort of citrus—mandarinas, clementinas, naval and juice oranges.

As Jaime and Renate ushered us inside the market to a hall full of cheese makers, we were introduced to several of the villagers who make cheese. Wood tables were laden with newly-made cheeses—hearty Cabrales blue cheese from caves in a neighboring town, small delicate fresh cheeses such as Afuega'l' Pitu. There were also tables full of Gamaneu, the cheese to which Jim and Renate had dedicated so many months of study.

As I tried to talk to a cheese maker named Christina (my Spanish is shaky at best), to my astonishment she introduced herself using fluent English! I asked her to tell me a little about herself and she said she perfected her English while earning a doctorate in education at Stanford University in California!

She explained that she grew up in Holland and attended undergraduate university in Amsterdam. It is another complicated story, but the gist of it is that she ended up in Asturias after living in southern Spain, where she enjoyed the experience of raising a few sheep and goats. Not wanting to raise the animals for slaughter, Christina decided to apply for a three-month apprenticeship in cheese making, held in Cangas de Onís. She so fell in love with the area and the people that she never left! Now she is tending animals and making cheese with her partner Pepitu, a local shepherd who proudly drove Ruth and me along a rutted muddy lane to show us their fold.

Pepitu led us across a green pasture to their corral, which contained frisky goats and their kids, heavy wool-coated sheep with their lambs, two substantial sheepdogs who protect the flocks and a Vietnamese pot-bellied sow with lots of piglets! He then demonstrated how he makes cheese, lightly smoking it with a little stove in a small wooden building. The cheese could not be more hand crafted.

What drew us all to this valley? For Ruth and me it was the myth of Covadonga. For Jaime and Renate, it was a return to his roots, the culture of the people and their artisan handiwork. For Christina it was learning how to make cheese and finding a rewarding life with her Asturian partner Pepitu and the community of shepherds.

What a remarkable juncture of lives! One small town tucked in a mountain valley harbors ancient dolmens that were objects of devotion 4,000–6,000 years ago. It also is saturated with the legends of Don Pelayo and Covadonga, as well as the towering figure of Santiago and the initial events of the Reconquista. Now kings and warriors are gone, and it is home once more to shepherds and cheese makers. Once in a while, Cangas de Onís hosts inquisitive outsiders who seek learn what she has to offer, if only for a few days or months.

Medina Sidonia:
Sweet Irony

When rival cultures intermingle for centuries, it can sometimes create ironic accidents. One of those accidents has a sweet flavor. The classic treats for Navidad, the celebration of Christ's birth, are Moorish (Islamic) confections. It is a happy natural convergence when people learn to live with one another.

Today, and for centuries past, the traditional Christmas treats served in Spanish homes have been variations of almonds, honey, and sugar, dating back to Moorish confections from Andalucía's Islamic era, and before that Damascus.

If you want to see where these sweets have been made for five or six hundred years, come with me to an unsung and unspoiled town where time stands still. We will take the road up the winding mountains to Medina Sidonia, a little known ancient hilltop town. It is one of the dramatic white towns that glisten in the blazing Mediterranean sun of Andalucía.

We will enter through the magnificent Arco de la Pastora, close to the road to Jerez de la Frontera. It is one of three gates built during Moorish times that lead to the Plaza de España, an elegant town square with well-tended gardens, flowers, palm trees, and places inviting you to sit and enjoy life.

Stately buildings embrace the plaza. The Ayuntamiento is the grandest—a Baroque and Neo-classical town hall with a magnificent Renaissance façade built in the seventeenth century. Nearby is the church of Santa María la Coronada, built on the foundations of the original castle and a mosque from Moorish times.

Everywhere is an Islamic emphasis on symmetry, flowing waters and flowers. Coming from a desert culture, it is their way of appreciating Creation.

The closest Christian approximation would be within a monastery with a peaceful cloister, inviting the faithful to meditate. (My favorite is the monastery of Santes Creus, near Tarragona, a seldom-visited treasure, overlooked by time and tourist.)

Many years ago I remember sitting in the square of Medina Sidonia under softly-waving palm trees with friends who had accompanied me from our language school in Cádiz. Soon we noticed that across the square was a type of bar/community- gathering place filled with older men who were passing the day playing dominoes together. My friend, a cheeky young English lady dentist, immediately strolled over to chat with them—entering their "sacred" space, and they were quite puzzled!

Quite close to the men were several pastelerías or sweet shops, laden with treats beyond our imagination. We have nothing like that in America, or even in the magnificent shops I have visited in the Netherlands, Germany and Belgium. The European shops do not have the wonderful confluence of two cultures: Moorish and Christian.

Amazed, we stood in front of the showcases looking at several-hundred types of sweets that were made for the townspeople, not tourists. The pastelerías in Medina Sidonia had all the tempting chocolate creations of Europe, but liberally sprinkled throughout were figuritas de mazapán, turrón, pan de Cádiz, and alfajores. The Moors were in southern Spain for almost 800 years (from 711 to 1492 AD), so it is no surprise that the confections have a Middle Eastern base: almonds, honey, olive oil, maybe a little egg, orange and other citrus essences.

The seemingly unlimited combinations produced by these few basic ingredients are remarkable. Pan de Cádiz is made of almonds, sugar, sweet potato, egg yolk, and cream. Mantecados include shortening, almonds and honey. Alfajores contain flour, extra-virgin olive oil, sugar, cinnamon, and sesame seeds.

This cheerful, unassuming village is believed by some to be the oldest city in Europe. It was an early Iberian settlement, Asido, conquered by the Carthaginians two centuries before the birth of Christ, and became known as the city of Sidon.

During Roman times, Medina was known as Asido Caesarino. I walked to one of the side streets, Calle Espíritu Santo 3, and saw some remarkable Roman cisterns that date from the first century. They stand over six feet high and are another example of great Roman engineering.

Arco de la Pastora, Medina Sidonia

The town was one of Spain's most important ducal seats in the fifteenth century, producing an admiral who led the Armada against England. The title of Duque de Medina Sidonia was bestowed in 1445 upon the family of Guzmán El Bueno for his valiant role in retaking the town from Moors. It is the oldest ducado in Spain, passed on without interruption through today.

Don Alonso Pérez de Guzmán became the seventh Duke of Medina-Sidonia in 1555 when his father died. He became master of one of the greatest fortunes in Europe. But in February 1588 his fortunes changed. The skilled naval leader Álvaro de Bazán died. Don Alonso was nominated in his place to command the Armada against England.

He protested forcefully that his appointment was inappropriate for this post, but Philip II would not hear of it. Regrettably, his inexperience and lack of seamanship were among the causes of the Armada's defeat by England. For some reason this did not diminish his reputation. Philip II appointed Don Alonso Captain General of the Ocean Sea in 1595. He remained in command of the Armada under Philip III—even though he presided over further catastrophes such as the sacking of Cádiz by the English the next year and the destruction of a squadron by the Dutch off Gibraltar in 1606.

Medina-Sidonia is a remarkable mountain town. As you stroll her streets you would never imagine her illustrious past. Home of Iberians, Carthaginians, Romans, Moors, Christian dukes and admirals, this tiny mountain town has seen it all, and welcomes you to an afternoon of repose before heading back to the twenty-first century.

What fun!

4
Fathers and Sons

King Juan Carlos talks with his son Prince Felipe

Farmer and King:
Mentoring Sons

A poignant image of forty years ago sticks in my mind. Ruth and I were exploring the back roads of rural Galicia. We were driving cautiously in this remote area of northwest Spain because often we would have to slow down, accommodating a farmer leading his oxen to the field. It was quite a scene: the weathered face of the man and the docile expression of the large beasts yoked together, with rabbit pelts between their horns to keep off flies.

This particular morning I noticed a farmer behind a horse-drawn plow, preparing a small patch of field. His son was by the father's side—he couldn't have been much older than seven. They were plowing the rocky field together. Sometimes the father would give the horse's reins to his son so that he would become familiar with that aspect of plowing. As they worked together over the hours, the father would share his thoughts and skills with his son—to help his boy to prepare for his adult role in life. Family traditions were being passed to the next generation in a very natural way.

About twenty years later, Ruth and I flew into Madrid hours after the attempted coup (golpe). Elements of the Guardia Civil had invaded the legislative chamber of the Cortes firing automatic weapons, and were holding about 350 members hostage. We had to gingerly weave our way through heavily armed men to reach our hotel room, located down the street from the parliament building! Inside the Cortes was high drama.

The king, Juan Carlos, had to choose between those who would enhance his power or the young democracy that was hanging by a thread. Many lives were in the balance. In the midst of the crisis that would define his place in history, the king called for his twelve-year-old son. Just as the farmer wanted to share his skills and thoughts with his son to prepare him for his role in life, so Juan Carlos wanted his son Felipe to learn what it was to be a king.

More than twenty years have passed since that fateful time. The bonding of father and son, king and prince, which started that critical night, has borne fruit. Spain has become the envy of Europe as a prospering democracy, and the nation celebrated a royal wedding where it shared in the pride of Juan Carlos and Sofía as their son Felipe married Letizia.

As I write this, Ruth and I enjoy watching our son Jonathan playing with Sarah, his four-year-old daughter. Even at this young age she learns from her father's love and experiences his values. Our son Tim loves to go fishing with his young sons, Sam and Ben. Tim teaches them how to get the bait, cast the line, and allows them to "take the reins" of the boat. These are precious times between fathers and their children.

What a joy it is to be a father and see your sons grow strong, as they themselves become husbands and fathers. Fathers provide a foundation for their children, whether they are farmers plowing fields, kings governing nations, or regular men teaching their children what they value in life.

Rafael Nadal, Rogers Cup 2008 (Toronto)

Son and Star

Rafael Nadal is a remarkable young man who, at the moment of his extraordinary triumph, reflected the time-honored values of traditional Spain. At the age of nineteen he won the French Open tennis tournament. After Rafael scored the winning serve he immediately rushed over to embrace his family—and then in his youthful exuberance he hugged Juan Carlos I, King of Spain!

During the post-tournament celebration, as he was speaking softly to his parents and other members of his family, he looked up at the press and said, "I hope all this won't change me. I would like to stay the same as I have always been, and I believe I will pull it off. I want to continue being a nineteen-year old youngster and play my tennis."

Six years later, I think he has pulled it off. In the scheme of things, Rafa's accomplishment is even more remarkable than all the subsequent tournament victories that have rocketed him to stardom. He is now the top tennis player in the world. After the glory days are over—fame is so transient—Rafa has a good chance to live a normal life on his own terms within his family and his neighborhood.

In the traditional Spanish family, children maintain an intimate connection with their families well into their adult lives. It is not uncommon for sons and daughters to remain at home until they are married in their late twenties. In the United States we have the understanding that if our children hang around home much beyond eighteen, it is time to nudge them out the door. We want them to become independent and self-sufficient.

Today some Spaniards discard the traditional way of life as old fashioned and stifling. But is it not a good thing when love between parents and their children is allowed to mature within the extended family? Apparently that is what the young tennis player believes. Rafa and his family have made a conscious decision to immunize him from the seduction of fame—to the extent this is possible in our media-saturated world.

Whenever you see Rafa in public he is well mannered and considerate, a clear indication that he was raised by a family with its priorities in order. Drawing on the experience of his uncle, who was a defender for three Spanish World Cup soccer teams, he has learned how to handle fame with grace. The structure of the Nadal family is traditional, in which the father is the head, and support among the family members is unquestioned. From the day he was born, Rafa has drawn strength from the men who have surrounded him.

His father's love has been unwavering. When Rafa suffered a stress fracture to his left ankle just as his career was ascending to new heights, his natural reaction was to return home. For the next three months his father devoted all his energy to his son's physical (and spiritual) recovery. Fully mended, Rafa returned to compete in the 2006 French Open, where he won the title from Roger Federer, the best tennis player in the world. Ecstatic and exhausted after the victory, he fell into his father's arms, saying, "Thank you, Papi."

His father's brother Antonio is the only coach Rafa has ever known. Uncle Toni has taught Rafa not only the fundamentals of tennis, but more important he has instructed his nephew in the fundamental values of life. Toni told one writer, "It's really easy for these guys to start thinking the world revolves around them. I never could have tolerated it if Rafael had become a good player and a bad example of a human being."

The Nadal family still lives in Manacor, as they have since the fourteenth century. It is situated on Mallorca, one of the Balearic Islands east of the Spanish mainland in the Mediterranean Sea. The Nadals own a four-story apartment complex that is the locus of the family. Rafa has his own apartment on the same floor as his younger sister's. In neighboring apartments are his mother and father, and his grandparents. Uncle Toni, his wife, and three daughters live there too.

Many Nadal men have great athletic ability. You might think that this would be a family of "jocks." But the family is more balanced. One of Rafa's grandfathers is a retired orchestra conductor. His father Sebastian is involved with real estate and a small business in town. Rafa relaxes by fishing with high school friends, and has continued to date the same hometown girl since he was nineteen.

Early in his career Rafa described himself as a "simple boy." He tells reporters that after his glory days are over he will still live in Mallorca. Of course he will have some role in sports, but he also will be active in a charitable foundation he and his mother have founded to help third-world children. In the meantime he lives happily in the present, aware that his career might last several years at the top of the game, or maybe not. When he retires he says he will buy a normal-size boat to go fishing from his island home.

I find it reassuring to know that in our fragmented society are the Nadals and hundreds of other Spanish families who live the alternative way of tradition. My father and his seven brothers and sisters lived in a similar way in Brookline, Massachusetts in the early twentieth century.

The present emphasis on autonomy, personal freedom and privacy (protected by irritating passwords!!) deprives many of us of a life of mutual support. I rarely see my cousins. Because of our travels, our sons have only a tenuous connection with theirs. I am not sure this is a good thing.

A major reason we enjoy our travels in Spain on behalf of La Tienda is the opportunity to visit the families among the small artisan producers who have become our friends. It brings meaning to our trips.

I have sometimes wondered whether I have over-romanticized traditional Spaniards and the values by which they order their lives, but when I learned about Rafael and his family, I knew my assessment was accurate. Traditional Spanish values produce a remarkable people.

The benchmark of Spanish culture is this warm and cordial hospitality extended to family members and guests alike. Our family experiences this generosity of spirit whenever we are with them—whether we are dining with jamón ibérico scientists from the University of Cáceres, or enjoying a cookout with a Spaniard in Greater Boston.

Best of all, this generous way of life can become contagious!

Tomás Lozano

Memories of a Shepherd Boy

In the early years of La Tienda, a young man named Tomás Lozano contacted me. At the time we were experimenting with many new products from Spain to discover what our customers would like. We featured ceramics, foods and some hand-carved reproductions of medieval art, including wooden panels and crosses. Tomás was calling to buy a polychrome cross as a gift for his wife Rima.

This was an unusual request from a young person raised in our secular age, and I was intrigued. As we talked over the phone at great length, I sensed that

Tomás and I shared a close affinity with the spirituality of medieval art and sculpture. Over the years our friendship has grown. We have come to know one another through emails and through my listening to a CD he made titled *Crisol Luz: Songs of the Middle Ages.*

Tomás playing with his father

Tomás with his father and cousin Carmen

Tomás's family is from a tiny town high in the mountains northeast of Granada. His grandfather was a miller who also owned a bakery, but it was confiscated during the Spanish Civil War. To be safe he withdrew with his family to operate a very remote mill in the country. He died when his son was fifteen, leaving Tomás's dad to take over the mill. On his mother's side, Tomás's family were farmers. When the Civil War started, her father was sent to the front and was only one of six survivors of a 200-man battalion.

During the sixties both families moved to the north seeking employment. Eventually they settled far from Andalucía in an industrial section of Barcelona, where manufacturing opened new possibilities. Tomás was born in 1967, and grew up speaking Spanish at home and Catalán outside of the house. He also learned French at an early age.

When Tomás reached his fifth birthday it was time for him to begin learning how to be a man. During the summer his parents entrusted him to his mother's uncle, who spent his life in the fields as a shepherd. In Cataluña, Tomás lived as a shepherd boy, tending sheep side by side with his great-uncle, and "grew strong in the fields," as Tomás describes it. He cherished those summers with his uncle, strolling through the meadows among the sheep and dogs, accompanied by birds that would perch in the tree groves around them. He and his uncle Francisco would take naps and eat ripe figs and plums off the trees.

If you will take a moment, I invite you to get to know Tomás, through the piece he wrote for liner notes from his CD, *The Morn of Saint John's Day*.

> I remember what Uncle Francisco taught me. He, like all good shepherds of his time, would sing during the long walks and waits in the fields, watching the sheep graze in green pastures and along riverbeds. He played no instrument, but made good use of his strong, rasping voice and whistles which, to a boy hardly three feet above the ground would frighten the wits out of me, so shrill and loud they were.
>
> He knew a great deal of stories, songs, sayings and old ballads. He was a repository of popular culture. Too bad that I, too young to know better, did not record his wealth of knowledge, gather it somehow, besides what rubbed off on me almost by osmosis. I cannot remember the songs, but my mother tells me that (they were) among a long list of ballads. By the time I had my wits about me, the shepherd and his sheep had long gone. Ballads form part of my life and also that of my

elders—farmers, millers and shepherds. My grandmother recited portions of the *Conde Olinos* to me as a boy and I especially remember an occasion when I fell asleep to the words, "That is not the little mermaid, mother nor the merman, but the son of the Kingly Count who for me is a wanting."

As Tomás progressed to higher grades of school he played Catalán folk music (including some from medieval days) with his fellow students. Soon they were playing in small clubs in Barcelona. His singing was particularly appealing because his traditional Andalucian roots enriched it.

In 1993 Tomás and his fellow performers were sponsored by a Spanish Ministry and invited to perform medieval and traditional music throughout North America. Their last performance was in New Mexico, where they became enchanted with its old Santa Fe families who spoke a beautiful old form of Spanish. They had been carrying on the traditions of Spain for generations.

Tomás was astonished to see traditions from old Spain still alive in the United States. He decided to stay a bit longer to experience this amazing place, and then a bit longer, until fourteen years passed before he moved on!

During those years Tomás and his friends created a series of theatrical and musical shows that they took to the schools of underserved communities. In some cases they were very small villages—rural and isolated areas with Hispanic towns and Native American communities. Many times they found that no one had ever before performed in their schools or community centers.

While Tomás was immersed in New Mexican traditions he met a soul mate and now wife, Rima Montoya, who was a graduate student at the University of New Mexico. Together they wrote a book, published in 2007 by the University of New Mexico Press, titled *Cantemos al Alba—Origins of Songs Sounds and Liturgical Dramas of Hispanic New Mexico*.

The most interesting thing that I learned from their research among colonial-era Franciscan manuscripts is that by 1629 (nine years after Plymouth Rock), there were full orchestras and choirs in the New Mexican missions, where the musicians and singers were Native Americans from the different pueblos. By 1654 most of the missions also had an organ. It is an important part of the American musical history that is completely missed.

Over the years I have grown to appreciate what a remarkable and humble man this shepherd boy has become as a singer, musician, scholar and writer.

Making sure that my memory was accurate before writing this reflection, I asked Tom for his recollection of our first contact:

> During the time that Rima and I were doing the investigation for *Cantemos al Alba*, I discovered an interesting web site that had lots of things from Spain, La Tienda. Back in 2002, they had beautiful reproductions of medieval carvings from Spain. I was very interested in getting one for my wife who was away visiting her family, and I wanted to surprise her in her return.
>
> I have always been in love with everything that has to do with the Romanesque. I don't know exactly why, maybe it is because of its harmony, or because I grew up surrounded by Romanesque towns that it is such a part of me. I called La Tienda and a gentle man answered the phone and almost instantaneously we had a great connection. That first conversation lasted an hour and a half. That man, to whom I hold a great friendship, even though we have never met in person yet, was Don Harris. This is a proof that human soul is beyond time and space.

As you can imagine, I am deeply touched by his remarks, and resonate with Tomás's love of the Romanesque. The architecture of the churches and monasteries reflect a sense of harmony, order and equilibrium, as did the Gregorian chants sung within them.

The bond Tomás and I felt has been a lasting one, yet we still have not met in person!

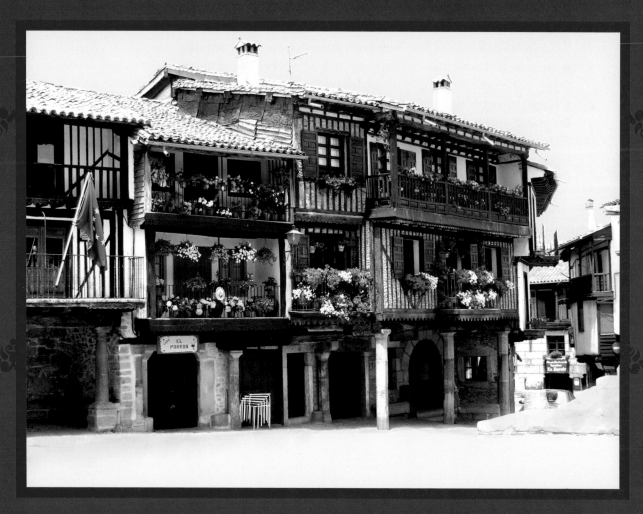

Plaza Mayor, La Alberca

5
Zarzuela (A Pot Pourri)

Roadside marker Camino de Santiago pilgrims

The Essence of Spain:
El Camino

If you wanted to travel off the beaten track in Spain to absorb the country's essence, where would you go? This is not an easy question to answer, since Spain includes many different peoples: ranging from redheaded men playing bagpipes in Galicia to dark-eyed señoritas in their flamenco dresses, riding sidesaddle at the ferias in Andalucía. Spain has seventeen autonomous regions, each with its own appeal.

Anyone's understanding of Spain is bound to be subjective. Since my family and I lived among the warm and gracious people of Andalucía, the region has a special place in my heart. I have images of the Giralda tower in Sevilla, the Alhambra palace and gardens of Granada, and la Mezquita, the Mosque of Córdoba. I recall pungent wine barrels in a sherry bodega next to our house, and the fishing boats bringing fresh seafood into the harbor. Andalucía is a fascinating part of Spain where Moorish and Christian cultures converged; nevertheless, it is only a piece in the Spanish mosaic.

There is one experience that embraces all of Spain, and that is to travel the pilgrimage route that begins in Northern Europe and leads to the holy city of Santiago de Compostela. The Camino is a pathway that people of all sorts and conditions have trod for well over a thousand years.

It spans from the snow-capped Pyrenees to the windswept shores of Celtic Galicia. There in the pilgrim city of Santiago de Compostela lie the bones of St. James, patron saint of Spain. For Spaniards, Santiago is the focus of the 700-year Reconquista of their land from the Moors. I have told that story in the essay "Covadonga: Tales of War and Cheese."

In medieval times, as today, pilgrims had many reasons for walking along the Road. From the furthest corners of Spain came penitents seeking to cleanse their sins at the cathedral's Door of Pardon. Others made the long and arduous trip as a means of personal renewal, exclusive of any miraculous claims. Artists and artisans offered their handiwork along the route and employed their skills as architects and stonemasons, adorning buildings, building bridges or constructing churches and monasteries.

The stream of humanity converged from all over Europe—people of many lands, languages and cultures. Charlemagne traversed the Camino, as did some of the people written about in Chaucer's Canterbury Tales. The travelers must have enjoyed many of the traditional products still around today, such as arrop, a medieval syrup made of pumpkin marinated in wine must; membrillo jelled quince sauce—quince was the European predecessor to the apple; various chorizos, sausages made of pork and smoked paprika; jamón and fig cakes.

Pilgrims walking along El Camino

While many consider walking the most authentic method for travelling the Camino, you can still catch its flavor by bicycle or car. Many times over the years, Ruth and I have wended our way by automobile through the many villages and small towns that sprang up along the path to serve the pilgrims.

We stayed in Santo Domingo de la Calzada in the same inn that St. Francis of Assisi visited. In León, we marveled at thousand-year-old frescos in the royal pantheon of the Collegiate church of San Isidoro. We were bathed in the pure light of the cathedral's amazing display of stained glass. We detoured from the main route to visit the Cámara Santa in Oviedo's cathedral, deep in Asturias. For me this is one of the most evocative and holy places of all.

The day without trails

Our son Jonathan walked the 400 miles across Spain in 1992. Along the way, he met many Spaniards from Aragón, Navarra, León, and El Bierzo. One man he befriended was a young itinerant Brazilian who had been in many parts of the globe on his personal pilgrimage. Years later, Jonathan would return to the Camino for his honeymoon.

Field of poppies along the Camino

In 1993 Ruth and I traveled to Santiago de Compostela to welcome Jonathan as he completed his walk, and to celebrate the feast day of St. James, the patron saint of Spain. It falls on the 25th of July, and when that day falls on a Sunday, as it did in 1993, it is a Holy Year with expanded celebrations. After a joyful reunion, the three of us blended into the warm and engaging crowd gathered in front of the pilgrimage cathedral. We stood among thousands of Spaniards from all walks of life, and from the varied regions of Spain. Included were pilgrims from across the globe.

Soon we were enveloped in a light show that was flashed upon the imposing façade of the cathedral. It celebrated the crucial victory of native Spaniards over the marauding Moorish troops of Al-Mansur. Their victory was a sequel to the Battle of Covadonga, which changed the course of Spanish history. The essence of the celebration was the affirmation of a common bond. Spaniards revisit their spiritual roots on this feast day of Santiago, Saint James, who led the emerging nation into battle.

When we founded La Tienda, our family wanted to reflect this unifying event of Spanish tradition by choosing the cockle shell of Santiago as our La Tienda trademark. For the same reason we selected the Peregrino (pilgrim) brand for our private label, with its shell and crossed walking staffs.

In America, there is an association named American Pilgrims on the Camino. It brings together people who have gained from the Santiago experience, or who are considering making the journey. Some of you might enjoy contacting them at their website, www.americanpilgrims.com. It is full of information, including aspects of spiritual retreat, and even training for those who want to return to the Camino to help other travelers on the Way.

What is the essence of Spain? Perhaps the pilgrimage is an apt metaphor, not only for Spain and its long struggle for unity, but also for each of us as we travel through life. Should you choose to mix with the townspeople along the Camino, you will experience the flavor of the centuries-old traditions of the Spanish people.

Bravery and Bulls

I could hardly believe my eyes. I saw a couple of brave young men vaulting over bulls in the middle of Ciudad Rodrigo. Turning to Ruth I said, "Isn't that what young men did in the Minoan culture thousands of years ago?"

We were sitting in makeshift stands erected for the running of the bulls in the plaza mayor, part of this agricultural town in Extremadura. This was no Hemingway bacchanal a la *The Sun Also Rises*—I did not catch a glimpse of Ava Gardner! Next to us on the rickety stands sat a couple of middle-aged farm wives catching up on the latest gossip. Close by was a family group drinking wine and carving slices of jamón from a leg they had brought with them. It felt like a community picnic.

We were witnessing an elemental rite of passage in which young men showed their valor before their approving neighbors by tangling with the bulls. I am no anthropologist, but it seems to me that this was an echo of the distant past. In prehistoric times bulls played an important part in the religious ceremonies of Iberian tribes living in Spain. Thousands of years ago during the time of the Minoan culture in Crete, the bull cult was central. We see evidence of the influence of bulls throughout the Iberian Peninsula, whether it be the cave paintings of Altamira, or the stone bulls of Las Arenas de San Pedro in Ávila.

Another echo of this ancient rite of passage into manhood is La Corrida, the miss-named "bullfight." In this ritual the bull, the essence of animal virility, is confronted and subdued by a sole human being, the torero, who is protected only by his faith, his valor and a thin sword. The magnificent toro bravo that he faces is an archaic strain of bulls that today is only preserved

Youths facing bulls, Plaza Mayor, Ciudad Rodrigo (Salamanca)

in Spain. Their ancestors were the primitive aurochs or urus, which once dwelled over wide parts of the ancient world.

Whether or not you approve of—or even understand—the corrida, it is a national tradition that many believe is the very essence of Spanish culture: a ritual that binds a historically-fragmented collection of regions into one country and that predates Spain itself. The corridas were even held in the midst of the bloody days of the Civil War!

"Our literature, our paintings, all of our artistic expressions are influenced by the world of the bull," one Spaniard observed, " It explains who we are." I think he is right. In what other country would you find huge black silhouettes of fighting bulls looming on the horizon as you wend your way through the rolling hills of the countryside?

Originally, it was a brilliant marketing strategy of the Osborne bodegas, makers of sherry and brandy in my "home town" of El Puerto de Santa María. Over much of Spain they installed colossal billboards cut in the shape of the bull with the word Osborne emblazoned in red letters across his body.

After Franco died, the reforming national legislature, the Cortes, passed sweeping legislation that included a ban on all roadside billboards. But the ink had barely dried on the document before they realized they had unintentionally done an unthinkable thing: the massive bulls would have to be removed from the landscape! So they went back into session and declared the bull silhouettes a national treasure, so long as the brand name was removed!

In 2005, many of Spain's mighty bulls were confined to the ranch under a quarantine aimed at halting the spread of a disease known as bluetongue. It is only harmful to sheep, not other livestock or humans. Still, it put the government in the unenviable position of trying to balance the interests of the fighting bulls, which represent a tradition that is nearly sacred in some parts of society, with the venerable sheep industry.

"The current measures would create the gravest crisis we have ever known," Enrique Garza Grau, secretary general of the National Association of Organizers of Bullfighting Spectacles, said in an interview. The gravest crisis? I know Spaniards often speak in hyperbole, but as I think about it, Señor Garza may not be far from the mark.

Galicia:
Salt of the Earth, Fruit of the Sea

The bond of the people of Galicia to their ocean is complete. The coast is punctuated by rías or fjords, fingers of the ocean reaching deep into the land, delivering the riches of the sea virtually to the doorsteps of their homes.

A large, bearded Gallego fisherman named Gaspar told my sons that not long ago the water was blackened by schools of fish. With a twinkle in his eye he bragged that he once caught a school of sardines in his swim trunks. Today, sardines and shellfish are at a fraction of historical highs.

Tim and Jonathan met Gaspar in the fishing village of Carril, located on one of the rías. The town is the site of Los Peperetes, the premium tinned shellfish of Spain. Their tiny plant is called Jelopa, named by the founder for his oldest son, Jesús Lorenzo Paz. It sits on the waterfront.

Across the street, one can see a small beach apportioned into small rock-lined squares of sand where the berberechos (cockles) and two types of clams are seeded and farmed. The shellfish grow in the top meter of sand with the berberechos on top, next a layer of almejas (clams), then another layer of a type of clams that are often eaten raw.

In 2008, Ruth and I decided to visit the specific area our sons had talked about so enthusiastically. We would "get away from it all" and spend a few winter days in the Rías Baixas (Lower Rías), the fjords of Galicia in northwest Spain. We packed wool clothes and rain gear, then embarked on our damp wintry adventure to the land of the Celts—which turned out to be no adventure at all!

Harbor at Laxe

As we flew into Santiago de Compostela and drove along the coast, visiting one sparkling fishing village after another, we passed dozens of acacia trees with bowers of gorgeous golden flowers. There were tall camellia trees (not bushes) filled with pink and white flowers. Once in a while, we would glimpse lemon trees so covered with their bright yellow fruit that we could not see a leaf. We experienced a pristine springtime as it was emerging.

One of our destinations was Finisterre (Finisterra)—finis terra—the end of the world. By the lighthouse on a rocky point of land we saw young pilgrims with their backpacks completing this last lap on the 400-mile-long Camino de Santiago, as pilgrims have done for more than 1,000 years. Then we went to the rival town of Muxía, which trumps Cabo Finisterre's claim as Europe's western-most land.

Muxía "one-ups" another famous town, Padrón. Padrón may have the little green pimientos de Padrón peppers and it may have been the site where the stone ship carrying the remains of Santiago (Saint James) from the Holy Land came to rest, but it was at the lighthouse of Muxía where the Virgen Mary stepped ashore from her own stone ship! The lighthouse El Faro Virgen de la Barca commemorates this. Should you think that stone ships do not float, you can visit a nearby Casa Rural and inspect one yourself!

Our trip was completely engaging as we visited one harbor after another along endless fingers of the fjords that run for hundreds of kilometers. We headed north along the "Costa de la Muerte" until the shore turned east along the Rías Altas (upper fjords). The shoreline is called the Coast of Death because of the high winds, turbulent waters and rocky coast where thousands of ships have met their fate—not the least of which were ships of the Spanish Armada, when 1500 sailors lost their lives.

At the northwest point is the village of San Andrés de Texeido. There young men gather as "maritime matadors." Rather than defying the magnificent virility of a fighting bull, they fearlessly confront the mysterious force of the ocean.

Between the ebb and flow of pounding surf they enter the ocean in small boats, approaching the jagged rocks where goose barnacles are firmly attached. With one ankle secured by a line to their dinghies, and a sharp knife held in their teeth, they slip into the surf at exactly the right time to approach the rocks.

Armed with sturdy blades they have time only to pry off a fistful of percebes, put them in bags tied to their waists, and hasten back to their boats. The small crafts must clear the shoals before the next pounding waves crash against the rocks. Every time these courageous fishermen go out to harvest the percebes, they know that the risk is high that they or their boats will be shattered against the rocks.

Local restaurants steam and serve percebes just as they are. Jonathan told me not to leave Galicia without enjoying some, even though the cost is astonishing ($80/lb). He was right. They have a pure taste of the sea—like Ipswich clams—but more so. I felt humbled by the brave men who risked so much to bring them to our table.

Many people first think of the exotic parts of Spain: flamenco, forts, fountains and colorful tiled patios. This legacy of 700 years of a Moorish presence is fascinating and significant. But the tapestry of Spain contains many more threads. Ruth and I find it absorbing to explore the variety of cultures still represented in this ancient land, including Celtic Spain—complete with bagpipes and the misty hills of the Northwest.

The next time you are planning a trip to Spain, I urge you to consider spending some time in green and gorgeous Galicia—especially in early spring before tourists come. The scenery is dramatic, the people are the salt of the earth, their crusty bread is astonishingly good, and the seafood is incomparable.

Tomb of the Lovers of Teruel

Los Amantes de Teruel: Unrequited Love

I would like to tell you of a wonderful Spanish tale of unrequited love.

On the western edge of the Maestrazgo Mountains is the fascinating town of Teruel. Because Valencia and the Mediterranean Sea are on the other side of the Maestrazgo range, Teruel has been a strategic location populated by Romans, Moors, El Cid, and many political refugees.

Tragically, much of the city was demolished during the Blizzard of 1937 in one of the most horrendous battles of the Spanish Civil War. But the town is resilient. Its stately Mudéjar towers stand tall with glistening ceramic-tile inlays and patterned brickwork. The winding streets of the Old Quarter retain a haunting Moorish flavor.

It was along these narrow streets in the early days of the thirteenth century that a knight named Diego de Marcilla neared the end of a five-year odyssey. He was exhausted from making the tortuous trek across the craggy mountains, yet his heart was filled with joy; for his journey had earned him the right to marry his beloved Isabel de Segura, and soon he would be in her arms. In fact, he heard wedding bells ringing as he approached his home town. He could hardly wait.

Diego and Isabel had been in love since they played together as little children. But when they matured into two young people deeply in love, Isabel's father, a wealthy merchant, was reluctant to bless their proposed union. As the second son of a noble family, Diego did not have the funds necessary to maintain Isabel in the style to which she had grown accustomed.

Isabel's father finally relented on one condition: the two could marry when Diego proved his noble lineage as a valorous knight, returning with enough wealth to give Isabel the life she deserved. "This must be accomplished within exactly five years," he warned, "no exceptions. If you meet the requirements, you can have the hand of my daughter Isabel in marriage. But if you fail, I will see that my daughter marries well into a prominent noble family."

The five years passed and Diego returned to Teruel in the prime of his youth—strong, handsome and wealthy. He was honored throughout the land for his courageous victories in many battles against the invading Moors. Confidently he awaited his reunion with his beloved.

But being the usual impulsive young man, he had not kept track of the time. The very day of his triumphant arrival in Teruel was the day the deadline expired. Soon he learned from friends that the wedding bells he heard were not for him and his beloved Isabel; they were for her marriage to another. Prudence and the enthusiasm of a very eligible (and noble) suitor prompted Isabel's father to delay not even one day before giving his daughter in marriage to Pedro Azagra, Lord of Albarracín. He had arranged a good marriage indeed.

Brave Diego was beside himself, filled with disappointment and rage. But he realized that it was his error; Isabel's father had kept his word. Crestfallen, he approached his beloved Isabel and tearfully told her he must leave her and the town of Teruel forever. He asked only for a farewell kiss. But it was not to be; for Isabel could not grant his wish (and her desire) since now she was wed to another. The full force of what happened confronted Diego, his heart literally burst. The brave knight crumpled to the floor, dying of a broken heart.

The wedding chimes tolled mournfully. The next day, as grief-stricken families and friends processed with Diego's body to the church, a young woman, her face veiled, slipped out from the file of mourners and silently approached the fallen knight. She kissed his cold mouth, offering the kiss she had denied him in life. At that moment, Isabel fainted and died in her lover's arms.

The place most visited in Teruel is the cathedral where a sublime marble monument carved by Juan de Ávalos portrays the two lovers buried side by side, their hands reaching out to one another. Diego and Isabel were real people. His true name was Juan Martínez de Marcilla. Her's was Isabel Segura.

When Do They Ever Sleep?

The Spanish people live in quite a different culture than ours, as many of you have experienced, even if you have only been to Spain for a few days. Rather than the home being their castle, the community is the focus of their lives. "Home is where I sleep," a Spanish friend of mine explained, "I live in my neighborhood."

In smaller towns on any given evening, you will see people of all ages strolling the streets together, making a "paseo." It is an inter-generational time when you might see older people walking with their children, and the younger generation, too. More often than not, the goal is a favorite café or bar they have been going to for years. There they will chat with old friends, cousins and neighbors. Small children play within sight of the older people.

My adult life in America is not at all like it would be in Spain, or even as it was when I was a child. As a little boy, I could play with the kids in my neighborhood for hours, come home for supper, and then go outside to play until it was dark. I liked the days of June especially. Not only was school over for the year, but the long hours of daylight suited me perfectly. It was sort of like Spain!

Now that I am older, I do not go out routinely to enjoy friends and neighbors. We may schedule a cookout or meet at an organized picnic—that is what our neighborhood did for Memorial Day. Maybe we go to a local concert on the lawn once in the summer. But we have lost that childhood freedom to go out into the neighborhood just to be with friends, as many of us did as kids. It is not customary in America.

The routine many of us follow in America precludes spontaneous contact with our neighbors. Part of the reason is that Americans move so often. The average is about once every seven years. So we, or our neighbors, may come and go before we get a chance to know each other. Another factor is that our extended family may be spread across hundreds of miles, so practically speaking the only family we see is under our roof.

The attitude of many suburban Americans is that our home is our castle. We get up in the morning, sometimes before sunrise, eat breakfast and individually drive to work. When the day is over many of us drive home, push the automatic garage door opener and safely park within the confines of the house. There we have dinner with the family, play with the children before putting them to bed, and then relax, perhaps watching a ball game or working in the yard. It is a nice way of life in many respects.

El Albaicín on a spring night, Granada

Most Americans are taken aback when they travel to Spain and discover that the normal time for the evening meal is about 10:00 PM. I am sure many of you have had the experience in Spain of feeling famished and going to a restaurant at a fashionably late 8:00 PM only to find the dining room empty!

Part of the reason for the late hour is the accident of time zones. If you look on the map, you will see that Spain is directly south of England and ought to be operating on Greenwich Mean Time. However, because the Iberian Peninsula is physically attached to Europe, it is more convenient for commerce to conform to European time, which is one hour later. In summer, Spain effectually operates on "double daylight savings time" where it is still daylight at 10:30 in the evening. Who wants to go to bed then? And so, Spaniards don't!

In traditional environments most Spaniards have an ample noon meal at 2:00 or 3:00 PM and may take an hour to eat, followed by a siesta. Stores are closed for several hours. After work (maybe 7:00 PM) it is time to be with friends and family at the local tapas bar. It may be close to 10:00 PM by the time they return home for a light supper.

Many young people then go out to socialize at discos into the wee hours. I remember one time we were "sleeping" in a small hotel in Valencia and the din of the merrymaking did not end until 3:00 AM! After the clatter produced by the bartender who emptied hundreds of empty bottles into bins by the street, there was finally some silence. To this day, I have not figured out when the Spaniards get any sleep!

When I was a young naval officer we lived in downtown El Puerto de Santa María among the sherry bodegas. We would often retire for the night hearing outside our window the laughter of young people and the rhythmic clapping of flamenco echoing down the cobblestone street. It took some adjusting to raise our little children when I had to begin work at 7:30 AM—a perfectly reasonable time for the Navy to start the workday when we were in Norfolk. I don't think adjustment to Spanish mores was high on the command's list of priorities!

In my early days touring Spain, I did not see any need to adjust at all. Touring was so efficient: everything conveniently halts in the middle of the day, and all the truck drivers dine at roadside cafes (and dining is the correct term, no quick hamburger for them). Nobody is on the road; museums are closed— what a great way to cover the country! This was my chance to speed to the next town on my itinerary, with a ham and cheese bocadillo in hand. I soon realized that I was observing Spain, without participating in the enjoyable way of life of the Spanish people.

In recent years we have learned to travel differently. We now enjoy the gracious rhythm of the culture. Rather than rocketing from town to town to see as much as we can, we slow down and stop to eat when the local people dine (including the truckers). It is a leisurely respite: good fresh salads and seafood cordially served by people who take pride in their service.

If we are in town, we find a popular café and allot an hour or two to enjoy life. Often people at other tables will acknowledge us as we join them in the restaurant—and say goodbye to all as they leave. Having a large meal at 3:00 PM leads to eating supper late at 10:00 PM, not 6:00 PM, which for the Spaniard is the mid-afternoon!

To appreciate people you need to be with them, adapting to their way of life. Ruth and I cannot think of a more pleasant time than sitting with friends, having a glass of manzanilla and some shellfish in the main plaza of Sanlúcar de Barrameda. Around us, life unfolds: we see young couples with their babies being fed caramelos by some delighted grandmother, pensioners basking in the sun, little boys and girls scampering gleefully around the central fountain.

America is not Spain, and our approach to life can be quite satisfying. We are mobile and individualistic, easily adaptable since our family roots are not as firmly planted in one location, as they would be in Spain. Just imagine a Spaniard coming to Colonial Williamsburg (where we live) and expecting dinner at 10:00 PM! I am afraid he would go away hungry. The place would be buttoned up for the night!

But we find that the two cultures are complementary. The great advantage of modern travel and communication is that we can learn from one another and have the best of both worlds.

Village dancers, celebration of Nuestra Señora del Pilar, Zaragoza

6

Fiestas and Celebrations

The Thrill of Valencia's Fallas

Valencia was my first port of call as a young Navy chaplain. Every chance I got, I would walk down the gangway to stroll the cobblestone streets of the Gothic Quarter. I enjoyed catching glimpses of what life in the historic port of Valencia has been like for centuries. At liberty call many of the young sailors, who were part of my destroyer squadron, would also explore the waterfront. Mariners have done this for as long as there have been seaports.

However this was not an ordinary port visit. We had tied up to the pier in time for the week of the fiesta of Las Fallas, and the people of Valencia were eager for us to become part of this fabulous event. You can imagine there was not much work being done aboard my U.S. Navy destroyer squadron—except for some poor unfortunates chipping paint or tending boilers.

When the rest of us went ashore, we found the air electric with excitement. All but essential work was already coming to a halt throughout the city, since virtually everyone in Valencia was involved in the fiesta, in one way or another. Many people had been preparing for Las Fallas all year long.

The Fallas fiesta of Valencia is an astonishing farewell to winter. Only those who have actually seen it can believe it. Some 700 fallas, large papier- mache monuments mounted over wooden frames, are burnt to cinders on the 19th of March—the festival of San José, patron saint of carpenters.

In the Middle Ages, as the days became shorter Valencian artisans and carpenters had to spend the last few hours of their workday laboring by the light of oil lamps. The lamps hung from crafted wood stands called parots. When spring arrived and days grew longer, the lamps and wood stands were no longer necessary. As part of spring-cleaning, the carpenters burned the parots, standing them up in the midst of wood shavings and scraps of lumber.

Over time the workers made a ritual of the event, adding an individual touch by festooning the lamp stands with rags and a hat. This evolved into a resemblance of a doll or human form. Such a figure, often depicting a person of authority in the neighborhood, came to be known as a ninot falla—fire doll. As the centuries passed, the local fires became spectacular blazes that still encompass the city every spring.

I spent my free time during the port visit strolling from one plaza to another. In one area I was attracted to clusters of people gathering in classic old stores with checkerboard marble floors. You know the ones—with mirrors on the walls like ice cream parlors had sixty years ago in America. Their parents and grandparents must have visited these same shops in their youth.

From several stores wafted the sweet aroma of fresh donut-like buñuelos (a native Valencian treat). Delighted revelers consumed them as fast as the pastries could be fried. In some shops, the buñuelos were served with horchata—a local cold white drink made of chufa nuts. Customers in other shops enjoyed the fresh pastries with wonderful thick hot chocolate a la taza. That was my choice.

The production of every falla (the monument, not the fiesta in general) is organized by falleros, a group of people from a specific barrio, or neighborhood. They are responsible for producing the falla and arranging their individual program so that everyone can join in the preparations. They hold meetings, pay dues, and seek sponsors to contribute money for their part of the festival. Throughout the months of preparation, they gather in a neighborhood clubhouse. On the walls are framed photographs and trophies they have earned in years past.

Neighborhoods compete with each other to build the most fantastic ninots (giant papier-mache images). The ninots are often grotesque dolls or figurines, made in a "wise-guy" tone, mocking local politicians, clergy, or others in authority. They can be several stories high, take months to build and in some cases cost over $100,000. A large number are on the "racy" side. A local Valencian remarked to my friend, author Penelope Casas, "You really have to be born and bred in Valencia to appreciate the bad taste of Las Fallas."

In contrast but integral to the fallas, are the falleras, young maidens dressed in traditional costume. Since Valencia proudly claims to be the only region in Spain that still weaves silk on manual looms, many young girls wear delicate damasks, brocades, and shawls of flowered silk intertwined with silver and gold thread.

Dressed in their finery, they process with baskets of flowers that they will present to Nuestra Señora de los Desamparados (Our Lady of the Homeless or Abandoned), the patron saint of Valencia.

During this time the square around the basilica is ablaze with color. The Plaza of the Virgin is transformed into a bower of flowers—even the façade of the basilica is carpeted with blooms. In the center is a huge fifty-foot image of the Virgin made completely of flowers.

The festival culminates in the eagerly anticipated crema (burning) on the night of San José, March 19, where hundreds of works of communal labor and artistry go up in smoke! By popular acclaim, one of the ninot comical figures is saved and placed in a ninot museum, a sort of Hall of Fame.

A crowd gathers at the Plaza del País. Smoke and haze have settled over the city from random fires and the gunpowder used in the rockets. Soon people become impatient with anticipation, and break into rhythmic applause followed by whistles and jeers as the hour passes, and there is still no crema, the final burning.

Suddenly all lights in the plaza are extinguished, and the crowd roars in approval. Fireworks illuminate the night—strings of firecrackers set off brilliant sparks, and colored rockets soar in the air, exploding thunderously. Over three hundred bonfires are lit throughout the city, and the noise produced by the accompanying fireworks is absolutely deafening.

Smoke and flames envelop every falla. As breezes blow and the air clears, the fire burns hot, and the heat is intense. The bases of the fallas are the last to ignite and in a flash, the structures collapse. After roars of approval, the crowd begins singing the Valencian anthem.

To tell the truth, none of the ship's company was around for the climax of Las Fallas, when hundreds of blazing structures light the sky. The commodore wisely decided to get our destroyers under way just before that day. The sailors had so much fun with the Valencians that they were physically exhausted. With this in mind, and a six-month deployment ahead, our admiral decided it was prudent for the crew to get some rest at sea! Therefore, I owe the description of the climactic events to others who have been there, including my good friend Penélope Casas.

While it is true that I did not experience every minute of las Fallas, the precious memories of my first days in Spain provided a lasting introduction to the warm and generous culture that I have since found throughout Spain.

Fervor and Fiesta:
Semana Santa and Romería

A while back I spent a month or two at a language school in the city of Cádiz, attempting to brush up on my Spanish (a daunting task!). My visit coincided with preparations of the townspeople for the celebration of their patron saint, Nuestra Señora del Rosario. They strung garlands of lights on the streets and constructed modest platforms for bands and other musical events. They were also assembling an exhibition that featured several floors of religious displays, including many golden crowns for the Virgin's brow and heavy jewel-encrusted capes for her to wear. There were different colors to match the liturgical calendar.

It was clear to me that people had made these items with religious devotion over the centuries, but as a man whose background is largely northern European, I was perplexed by what I was seeing before my eyes. I turned to my Spanish companion and said, "I wonder what this splendor has to do with the simple maiden of Nazareth?" He replied with an incredulous expression on his face, "Nothing directly, I guess. But this is our celebration and the Church exists for fiestas!"

It is this juxtaposition of fervor and fiesta that is so very Spanish. You can see it in baroque and rococo churches, and you can see it on the street. The religious component of celebrating their patron saint is swept into the people's elemental exuberance and spontaneity. Somber and pious religious expressions and prayers were not the dominant theme of the feast day, although I am sure this was part of it for many, and central for the devout.

Another time Ruth and I witnessed a Semana Santa procession in the ancient city of Zamora in Old Castile. Hundreds of men, some with their

Plaza Mayor, El Rocío (Huelva)

young sons, wound their way through the streets of medieval Zamora. Some joined together to carry massive mahogany pasos (floats) depicting the last days of Jesus' life. Many displays were so heavy that it took fifty men of the brotherhood to carry them haltingly along the processional path. The five-hour penitential march of the brotherhood cast a somber tone.

But halfway through their journey they stopped the procession in a park near the cathedral, took off their hoods and enjoyed a picnic with friends who brought some bocadillo sandwiches, a chunk of cheese and bottle of the local wine. Refreshed, they donned their hoods, hoisted the pasos and continued their profound procession! (You can read more about this ritual in "Semana Santa in Zamora.") As in Cádiz, the line between the fervor of their faith and their love of life and community was blurred. Secular and sacred were part of a whole piece.

Perhaps the most vivid example of this merger of fervor and fiesta is the Romería del Rocío, an amazing pilgrimage to a marshland village of Rocío outside of Almonte, where the Virgen del Rocío resides at her Ermita, a remote shrine or hermitage. This massive migration of people every spring stretches back into the mists of time. The current annual pilgrimage dates back 800 years.

Almonte is a small pueblo most of the year, but somehow they find room for nearly one million pilgrims every spring at Pentecost. It is located close to the Atlantic Ocean, southeast of Sevilla and adjacent to the wildlife preserve of El Coto Doñana.

Every year on the weekend of the feast of Pentecost (late May, early June), the road to the Ermita is packed with horses and decorated carriages that travel to the sound of music and drums. Pilgrims (romeros) come from all over Andalucía on foot, on horseback or by cart. No motorized vehicles used to be permitted. Most pilgrims wear traditional clothes: women in bright gypsy-inspired flamenco dresses and men in the unique wide-brimmed bolero hats and short-cropped jackets associated with Andalucía. As they get closer to Almonte, the pilgrims camp out in the fields and forests of the surrounding Doñana National Park.

The town has broad unpaved streets, with hitching posts by many houses. Hoofs generate the only traffic noise you hear. Some horses are classic Andaluz stallions with flowing manes and braided tails. Among the regular horses are white Lipizzaners, similar to those trained at the Spanish Riding School in neighboring Jerez de la Frontera.

Faithful oxen strain to haul wagons that carry the Madonna's simpecado, elaborate silver and gold altarpieces, brought from the churches of nearly one hundred Hermandades (brotherhoods) who make up the majority of the pilgrims. They are devoted to the Virgin of el Rocío and make their way to her Ermita. Elders of each brotherhood take the lead, riding four abreast. They are followed by their town's simpecado. A surging throng of faithful is last—clapping, chanting and beating drums.

While this unfolds, another type of romero is arriving. Hundreds of tour buses deliver bands of the faithful from all walks of life. They come from parishes across Andalucía and beyond. Although these pilgrims become part of the festive atmosphere, prancing stallions are of secondary interest. Prayerful piety is the focus of their journey.

On Pentecost Sunday, mass is celebrated for the throng of people who have migrated to the plaza in front of the church where the miraculous statue of the Virgin resides during the rest of the year. Later that night the culmination of el Rocío occurs within the Ermita, the resting place of the venerated statue of the Virgin, "La Blanca Paloma"—the Dove. As they do every year, the young men of Almonte jump over the iron railing that demarcates the sanctuary and hoist the image of the Virgin onto their shoulders. As they process through the village, many ecstatic faithful reach out toward Nuestra Señora del Rocío; some young mothers reach out over the enthusiastic crowd to have their babies touched by the Virgin.

For this brief moment, the panorama at el Rocío contains elements of a camp-out for hikers, family reunion, site for fervid devotion, and carnival. The crowds sing traditional songs and dance the sevillanas together in the fields. Sometimes you will hear soulful flamenco saetas from a man or woman overcome with emotion.

Wedges of Spanish tortilla, slices of jamón serrano, plates of langostinos and other shell fish, and sizzling fried peppers are sold, accompanied by plenty of refreshing manzanilla sherry and other local wines. Many pilgrims bless themselves by dipping their hats in water and anointing themselves. El Rocío is of one piece, not to be evaluated separately. In a day or so, the crowds will disperse and the fields of el Rocío will become quiet again.

Traditional Spain is another world, an ancient culture where continuity and variety are one. It is so different from our very young America, formed by waves of disparate people from every corner of the world. It is hard for the imagination of Americans to capture the elements of fervor and fiesta that are inextricably combined in Spain, unless we are willing to immerse ourselves in the event; or better still, allow ourselves the freedom of participating in an ancient culture.

Medieval Carnival in Cádiz

Cádiz is a beautiful sun-drenched port situated on a dramatically narrow spit of land. Within the medieval walls that separate its ancient winding streets from the modern world, Ruth and I welcomed in the millennium. Our celebration in Cádiz was so magical that we returned in 2001 to participate in its legendary Carnaval, which has been occurring for centuries, even in the most difficult times. (There have been a few interruptions, such as when Franco prohibited all Carnaval celebrations. In fact, Carnaval did not return in it's true version until 1977.) We spent three delightful days there—even staying up all night in the streets as we enjoyed the revelers in their inventive costumes. There were lots of moros, zorros and knights.

The unique feature of Carnaval is the musical fraternities. Groups of men, young and old, rove the cobblestone streets of this ancient seaport, singing satirical and entertaining songs based on events of the day. One group we saw was dressed as the First U.S. Cavalry, with packs of Marlboros in their holsters rather than pistols! References to Monica Lewinsky punctuated their satirical songs.

For the rest of the year, the men sing together weekly in their neighborhood clubs, perfecting their musical presentation for the next Carnaval, and enjoying each other's company over a glass of beer or manzanilla.

In 2009 we decided to return to the Carnaval to see how durable the tradition is, battered as it is by the storms of post-modernity that are sweeping across the kingdom. Since 2001, many more young women have left home for the workforce, and the peseta has given way to the euro—leading to unparalleled wealth from what was then a booming economy. This set the stage for a radical political shift that has dismantled many long-established social restrictions, such as abortion, divorce, and homosexual behavior. With such

Don and Ruth Harris with frightening Norsepersons, Carnaval de Cádiz

a tumult of change, we wondered whether the traditional values of the Cádiz community were still intact.

What did we find when we revisited the Carnaval eight years later? We found a resilient and prosperous people who are learning to redefine their social boundaries. Some of the traditional social restraint has weakened, but essentially the traditional Carnaval of Cádiz remains intact. Spain has absorbed many waves of culture, and has been the richer for it. I am hopeful that this age-old society, steeped in the traditions of family and community, will emerge intact, strengthened by modern experience.

We live in changing times, more far-reaching than we realize. To appreciate fully the solemnity of Semana Santa (Holy Week), the gaiety of Carnaval, and even the ritual of the bull ring, I think it is important to place these events within the context of the rural society from which they came. There are people alive in the villages of Spain who still recall the vanishing way of life that prevailed for well over a thousand years.

A benchmark that helped me make the mental shift to a pre-industrial mindset was the astonishingly beautiful and profound movie *Tree of Wooden Clogs* that I picked up on Netflix.com. It is a poignant look at European rural life a century ago, and the hardships facing three families as they bonded together to survive. A masterpiece filmed in Italy, it could just as easily have been filmed in Spain. I urge you to see it.

Two realities portrayed in the film stood out for me. First, I realized how fully communal was the life of these people, in the best sense of the word. They were their brother's keeper, working together long and hard to make their lives worthwhile in an unrelenting environment.

Their only respite was when the families came in from the fields and their chores to gather around the fireplace while a grandfather or another elder would delight the children with tales and ghost stories. They were people who, without a second thought, included even the lame and mentally disabled within their family circle. Our insistence on personal autonomy and individual rights would have been incomprehensible to them.

The second reality that became clear to me was how tied they were to the natural order of the seasons: planting, tending, harvesting and resting before the cycle began once more. They had no time for dreams of social mobility. There was no "time" at all, as we think of it: no clocks marking hours and minutes, just sunrise to sunset. Their unquestioning faith sustained them. Their local parish provided the markers of life: Baptism, First Communion, Matrimony, Advent, Christmas, Lent, and Easter. There was no omnipresent electronic clock, which is as close to us as our cell phone, or this computer.

In this context, Carnaval was not merely a party event for an individual's amusement. Everyone in the community was celebrating their mutual survival after another hard winter. They could see new life beginning to sprout from the earth. After forty days of Lenten preparation they would participate in the great festival of the Resurrection that focused on new life and hope, as reflected in the abundance of spring flowers.

Certainly the waning of the winter months was an excuse for merriment and joy—a big blowout, a sigh of relief. But it was always in terms of the community, not the individual. The traditional concept of the Carnaval in Cádiz is not a no-holds barred time to "raise Cain" and vomit in the street. Instead,

Revelers, Carnaval de Cádiz

even today, you will see as we did, random groups strolling down the winding streets, singing together; or people from a neighborhood coordinating the costumes they wear.

I am not a utopian or a romantic. Not for a minute would I like to trade the opportunities for individual growth that we have today. After all, Ruth's and my grandparents were emigrants who left their home countries in order to improve their lives—and those of their children. But, as with everything, this freedom has been bought at a price: individualism and mobility can fray family ties.

During times of less plenty, we in America are learning once more the virtues of taking care of one another. One indication in our country is that more parents are living closer to their grown children and their families. Now that the boom is over, I expect young Spaniards, who left home to be on their own, will renew their appreciation of their family culture.

The Easter Drums of Aragón

In 2004 I was at a friend's house in Spain, leafing through a European issue of *Time Magazine*. The cover story trumpeted "Spain Rocks!" Shaking off its benighted past, the author bragged, Spain was rising like a phoenix. This vibrant "new" nation was setting an innovative, dazzling standard for all of Europe. Her chefs were the talk of the world of cuisine; her people were dominating the worlds of fashion, music and the fine arts. Spain was at the vanguard.

But then I looked up from my magazine, and saw images flashing on the television screen—terrorists had just bombed the train station in Madrid. March 11 in Madrid was a painful echo of September 11 in Washington and New York thirty-one months earlier.

Since that terrorist bombing, Spain has exploded with radical social and political changes, discounting traditional values as "old hat," and in many ways mimicking the values of contemporary Europe. Traditional values had been slowly fading since the late 1980s, when the economic boom began. The bombing served as a catalyst for more radical change. The shift is quite astonishing, and in some ways disturbing. Yet I find comfort knowing that over the ages Spain has been able to absorb many passing influences while remaining anchored in her identity.

Some Spaniards who are less intoxicated with modernity are beginning to explore long-ignored cultural sites. By revisiting traditions and rituals they are seeking to understand their roots. It is this fresh appreciation of lasting traditions that will continue to anchor and define Spain for the next generation.

The central ritual of Spain focuses on Holy Week. Throughout this diverse nation, everyone—young and old, believer and skeptic—is drawn into the observance.

There is one Holy Week ritual that I hope to experience in the next few years. It takes place among a cluster of small villages deep in the mountains of Aragón. Once a year, all the inhabitants gather around their parish churches, take up their drums, form bands and spontaneously start drumming. For about twenty-four hours without pause, bands of drummers (largely young men, but also young women and a few children) process through the streets of their towns.

It begins on Good Friday as the clock of the parish church in each village strikes noon. An enormous roar resounds through the town as all the drums roll simultaneously. There are all kinds; traditional bass drums stretched with skin, modern snare drums, and many other types in between. The drummers dress in blue, violet or black gowns and hoods, the color depending on the custom of the village. They remain together for two hours, generating among their neighbors an indefinable emotion, which some describe as ecstasy. The drumming makes the ground tremble under their feet. When people put their hands on the wall of their houses they feel the vibration in their bones.

Then the townspeople form a procession, intermingling between the bands of drummers. They leave the Plaza Mayor and weave through their villages, finally returning to where they began. There are so many people who join the procession that the last have not begun before the first reach their goal.

In the procession are men and boys dressed as Roman soldiers; others (including little children) are centurions. There is a Roman general accompanied by men called Longinos, those who guarded the sealed tomb of Jesus. The drum rolls have five or six different rhythms. When two groups of drummers with differing rhythms encounter each other at a street corner, they meet frente a frente—face to face—and embark on a duel of rhythms. The contest can go on for an hour or more until finally one group acquiesces and assumes the rhythm of the stronger.

At about five o'clock the procession through the village is complete and the faithful pause in silence at the church, mourning the Crucifixion. Then the rolls of the drums sound in unison once more, and continue their distinct rhythm until the afternoon of the following day.

All night the townspeople are engulfed by the prolonged rhythm of the drums. By sunrise, some drummers have bleeding hands, but they continue throughout Saturday morning until they hear the sound of a trumpet as the church bell tolls the appointed hour. At that moment all drummers silence their drums. They will not play again until the next year. But for weeks after, some say the rhythm of the drums is reflected in the conversational pattern of the villagers.

Romans, Goths, Arians, Moors, Jews, Christians, and pagans before them—they have all contributed to the consciousness of these isolated towns. These various civilizations are woven into the rich fabric of Spain, and that fabric is lasting. I am confident that no terrorists of any stripe are going to change the traditions of Spain. Neither will the latest trends of Europe. Spain will continue to absorb the contributions of others. Her traditional values are not static, but they will endure.

Semana Santa in Zamora

A unique beauty surrounds the ancient city of Zamora when they celebrate Semana Santa. Their Holy Week is an occasion that is very genuine and very somber.

Zamora is an agricultural city with roots in the soil. Their vineyards provide some of the finest wine in Spain, and their sheep's milk produces the excellent zamorano cheese. Located in northwest Spain near the Portuguese border, Zamora's stone battlements remain as witness to the many key conflicts that affected the history of Castile, León and Spain as a nation.

Ruth and I traveled there in 2007 to experience Holy Week. When we arrived, the sincerity of the people was unmistakable. Semana Santa was a serious event in their lives. As an act of humility, some chose to walk barefoot during the processions. Yet we experienced something more: the power of an all-absorbing tradition as the entire citizenry worked in concert to express the values they share.

The strength and tradition of Zamora is reflected in this weeklong observance of Jesus' last days on earth. This central event mobilizes the city's life. Various merchants provide artfully-designed guidebooks and pamphlets so that observers of Semana Santa will know exactly where each procession begins, and the route that each will follow. Most processions consist of men and boys. Women and their daughters walk only once—on the eve of Good Friday.

All processions pass through narrow cobblestone streets within the city walls. One very dramatic procession winds its way from the fortified cliffs down to the riverbank, passing by a medieval bridge that lies near remnants of a Roman-built bridge. It is a particularly solemn procession, with incense, subdued drums, and music in a minor key.

Semana Santa: Carved paso progressing through the streets of Zamora

Ruth and I had hardly dropped off our suitcases before we were caught up in the drama of Holy Week. Before we knew it, we were involved in a profound ritual enacted annually for over a thousand years. Hundreds of men and boys were filing down the main boulevard, clothed in penitential robes and hoods, carrying long flickering tapers.

The focal point of every procession of men is the paso, carried by members of the confraternity. A large hardwood platform displays a hand-carved, life-sized tableau that represents one of the mysteries of the last days of Jesus' life. It is lifted up on the backs of forty or fifty strong men, and carried for many hours along the narrow streets with barely a pause. The rest of the penitentes accompany their paso wearing robes and hoods in colors unique to their brotherhood.

My wife and I were amazed to see that a few fathers had their very young sons walking by their sides in robes—some less than five years old!

Now and then we saw a typically Spanish touch. If we looked closely, we could see a man in the procession discreetly slipping caramelos (wrapped candies) to the children in the crowd!

One of the longest processions involves a route of many miles. Over five thousand men and a few young boys escort several dramatic hand-carved pasos as they pass through almost every neighborhood in the city. You can imagine the sight of all those men of Zamora in somber procession.

We were beginning to wonder how these people could survive such a long ordeal when, with a perfect Spanish touch, the procession ground to a halt in the Cathedral plaza. The men lowered their pasos, removed their hoods, and enjoyed an informal merienda (picnic) with friends and family; perhaps a chunk of chorizo, some sheep's milk Zamorano cheese, and a little wine brought from home. Suitably refreshed, they donned their hoods, hoisted their pasos and continued on their penitential path.

What impressed me most was that virtually every person in this small city, from toddlers to pensioners, participates in this community event every year of their lives. On Maundy Thursday night before Good Friday is a climactic procession involving thousands of men and boys who walk silently all night through the winding cobblestone streets of Zamora. Later, in the dusk of Good Friday, over four thousand women and their daughters process together in candlelight accompanied by a small brass band. There are no pasos in the women's procession. On Easter morning joyous townspeople fill the Plaza Mayor to witness the climactic procession of the Resurrection.

This is the power of tradition. It provides a unity of spirit among the people of Zamora. Everyone is involved. On Easter Sunday we were moved by the sprays of lilies and early spring flowers adorning the pasos for the Resurrection and the Virgin. We savored steaming sopa de ajo (garlic soup) prepared by the bartender of a neighborhood café and served in commemorative terra cotta cups. We rarely saw anybody but Spaniards. Clearly, this was not a tourist production.

In many ways there is nothing we do in America that parallels this Holy Week celebration that takes place throughout Spain. We have neither the

Penitentito—young boy processing during Semana Santa (Zamora)

centuries of tradition, nor in most cases, the stability of families living in one place for many generations. Nevertheless, we do have a flavor of this kind of community solidarity.

I am sure some of you have experienced the kind of common effort that small towns in rural America still expend to create an old-fashioned Fourth of July celebration. I know many of our friends, their children, and grandchildren have lined the streets of our hometown of Williamsburg and neighboring Yorktown waving flags and eating hot dogs.

As in Zamora, the prime focus is on a parade that involves local people representing various groups devoted to service such as the Red Cross or the Kiwanis. Marching alongside are civic leaders, school bands, veterans of past wars and perhaps small contingents of soldiers from the National Guard and other uniformed services— just as in Zamora.

To be sure, I am not equating a patriotic parade with a religious event in terms of the values they represent. However, I am saying that when people come together in a common enterprise devoted to commemorating the values they hold dear, there is a certain health and strength that sustains them long after the parade or procession is over, and the marchers go home.

Feria de Sevilla:
An Extraordinary Bonding

Late spring is an especially gentle time in Andalucía. If there has been enough rain in the winter the rolling hills, which stretch to the horizon with countless rows of olive trees, are blanketed with wild flowers that punctuate the soft grass. The starkness of Holy Week processions is but a memory in the many small towns and larger cities.

The Feria de Abril (Spring Fair) of Sevilla is an extraordinary event that occurs every spring along the banks of the Guadalquivir River. Thousands of sevillanos gather at their family casetas (canvas booths or pavilions) for a week with their extended family, many of whom are dear friends. Essentially the fair is a celebration of family, where the people of Sevilla renew the family ties that are the foundation of the Spanish spirit. It is also a time to celebrate spring.

The feria's centerpiece is dancing: young and old dance the sevillanas. It is inspired by flamenco, but simple enough that grandmothers can spontaneously dance with their sons or daughters-in-law. Husbands dance the sevillanas with their wives; nephews with nieces—even invited guests can join. No one is permitted to refuse an invitation to dance, and Jonathan fit right in, dancing with our hostess.

Within the family tent, the women are dressed in colorful flamenco dresses and the men in coat and tie. It is a time to catch up on the latest news from an out-of-town cousin or aunt, or spend time with parents, brothers and sisters, as well as entertain friends (such as Jonathan and me).

Since it is Spain, the bar at the back of each caseta is a cornucopia of delightful tapas: simmering garlic shrimp served with picos bread sticks, lightly-fried boquerones (fresh anchovies), glistening slivers of jamón ibérico; calamares, langostinos, fresh cracked olives, manchego cheese and almonds—the menu seems endless.

Family in front of a caseta at Feria de Abril in Sevilla.

For me, most precious of all was to see little children, mostly girls in flamenco dresses, perfecting their sevillanas technique with each other. Some were under four years old! In the caseta of our hosts Fernando and Sarah a flamenco guitarist played and sang while all ages of the extended family danced together.

Until 8:00 PM, families in horse-drawn carriages promenade down the unpaved avenues outside hundreds of family casetas. Also riding by are young men sitting upright on their handsome local horses, sometimes with señoritas riding pillion behind them.

Lest you get caught up in the romance and miss the point I am making, the feria is not a tourist event; it is a vast family reunion. If you did not know anyone with a family caseta you would be alone in the passing crowd. These family connections are so important that the city of Sevilla all but shuts down for a week so that people can get together.

Father and son

All girls love horses!
Feria de Abril, Sevilla

Cell phones are everywhere

Cousins at the feria

Whether in Spain or America, it is no secret that a child nurtured in a solidly committed extended family is set to thrive. The many traditional Spaniards we met in Sevilla had not been distracted from this truth.

When I stepped ashore more than forty years ago, I was attracted by the way Spanish people cherished their children, as well as they way they embraced all of their family. Much has happened since then. Spain is now a thriving new democracy with unprecedented years of material prosperity. Has the country changed? Of course it has. But for all the ephemeral glamour that Spaniards are enjoying in this era of unprecedented prosperity, Jonathan and I found in the Feria de Sevilla an affirmation of the family that is the bedrock of Spain.

Mother and Child

We can all recall a time when we have looked in awe at a precious, fragile newborn child, perhaps our own, or a cherished grandchild. No matter what our background, the tender image of a mother cradling the newborn infant reflects hope and life, and recalls the joy of loving families. It is a universal, fundamental emotion.

The image of mother and child is also the central theme of Christmas, Navidad—the birth. It is why "Silent Night" is the all-time favorite carol: "All is calm, all is bright/mother and child . . . sleep in heavenly peace." With Christians everywhere, the faithful in Spain celebrate the light of God's love in the person of a newborn child.

The centrality of a mother's love and the preciousness of her child are reflected throughout Spanish culture, where children are central to everyday life. Even families out for dinner at 11:00 PM have their children playing near the table. Children are so central to the family that it is not unusual in a traditional Spanish home to find sons and daughters living at home well into their twenties, as I discussed in "Son and Star."

I understand there are similar cultures around the Mediterranean, where mothers and children have a unique place, but I have not experienced them first hand. However I am well aware of cultures where the sanctity of the child is not emphasized; where children are to be "seen and not heard."

The difficulty now is that the cultures of America and Spain (to a lesser extent) have evolved into a two-income family structure; sometimes by choice, as mothers pursue personal careers and other times because of economic necessity. The result is that many of us are unable to replicate the traditional home. But with dedication and commitment our children can be assured of their value.

This is why the December holiday season is so important. It is a time for us to enter into their world as best we can. Whether or not there is a religious setting such as Christmas or Chanukah, parents enjoying time with their children within the extended family is a deeply spiritual occasion. During this time of year there is a natural human tendency to want to be closer together—to share each other's warmth and hopes. That is why this is the season for children, and has been since antiquity. In their joyful play and tender interactions they are oblivious to the long shadows. Children are pure life—as any grandparent understands most fully.

One of the nice things about Spanish culture, and some Eastern Mediterranean countries, is that all twelve days of Christmas are celebrated, leading up to Three Kings Day, el Día de los Reyes, on January 6. Their Christmas is not our abbreviated time leading up to an explosion of presents on December 25, followed by a rush to capitalize on the huge sales the next day!

During the several days and evenings after Christmas, Spanish families stop by the homes of uncles and aunts, grandparents and cousins to enjoy each other's company while the little ones—cousins and brothers and sisters—are having a good time together. A few slices of jamón and a table full of holiday sweets: polvorones, mantecados, mazapán and other delicacies unique to the season make it a warm and welcoming occasion for visiting family members. (You can read more about these Christmas sweets in the essay "Christmas Confections and Suffering Quince.")

I hope you have the opportunity to spend time with children, whether they are toddlers or soon to be young men and women. Time flies, and soon they will be on their way to discover the world. So don't miss a moment while you can. Even grandchildren grow up! But they are so much fun as you see them view life with wonder. We have two granddaughters, ages three and seven, and two grandsons, ages seven and nine. It is such fun to see them play together, and to see their uncles, aunts and parents in action.

"Monaguillo tocando la zambomba," Ignacio Pinazo Camarlench
Oil on canvas; 1893-95; Museo de Bellas Artes de Valencia

Zambomba:
Christmas in Jerez de la Frontera

As I've mentioned in other essays, since the 2004 bombing in the Madrid railway station there has been a radical political, cultural and social revolution in Spain. Traditional norms have been discounted in a carefree manner as Spain is intoxicated by its new position in the modern world.

Nevertheless I sense fidelity in the Spanish soul that transcends the various twists and turns of fortune. This constancy is revisited every year during the Christmas season, when Spaniards gather to renew their familial and cultural roots. Of course, Spaniards hold this in common with other people who have hallowed pasts. Often cultural centering is expressed in rituals such as the Seder, the Roman Mass, Orthodox Liturgy and the Muslim Call to Prayer.

I asked my dear friend Isabela Díaz what Christmas holidays were like in Jerez de la Frontera before the bomb rocked Spain. The Harris and Díaz families have known each other for more than thirty years. I first met Isabela's husband Pedro in a Spanish class he was teaching on the Base Naval de Rota. (You can read more about the Díaz family in "The Shoemaker's Son and Carpenter's Daughter.")

She told me that when she was a little girl some seventy years ago, there was no tinsel, Santa, Rudolph and Christmas trees—all of which have insinuated themselves into commercial Spanish culture. In the "good old days" a typical Jerez celebration for the evening of Nochebuena (Christmas Eve) was called Zambomba.

Originally Zambomba was celebrated in the houses where more than one family lived (casas de vecinos). Neighbors would gather in the downstairs patio around a fire set inside an oil drum and sing "villancicos flamencos," the traditional Christmas songs from Jerez. (Remember in that time neighbors knew each other for a lifetime since nobody moved away.)

Some of the neighbors would accompany the singing with improvised musical instruments, which were made of whatever material was available:

• Zambomba, a drum-like instrument made of a terracotta jar covered on the top with an animal skin. The skin had a central hole through which a long stick was inserted. The stick rubbed against the stretched skin, producing a deep sound. Periodically the skin was moistened with water so that it would remain flexible.

  • Tambourines, or similar shapes with small pairs of cymbals attached
  • Almirez, a brass mortar with pestle taken from the kitchen
  • An anisette bottle swept with a spoon

The music accompanied singing and clapping of complex flamenco rhythms that have echoes of Moorish Al-Andalus. A Christian celebration enhanced by a bit of the Muslim past—I love it!

One or two of the neighbors offered the group some drinks such as anisette or wine, and some snacks or tapas, as the others spontaneously sang Christmas songs flamenco style. Today, Zambombas have evolved into a more massive celebration in neighborhood squares, bars and even clubs. People still sing "villancicos" and pass around drinks and snacks but, Isabela assured me, they do not light up fires in bars!

Here is a traditional menu of typical foods jerezanos serve for Christmas Eve, Christmas Day and New Year's celebrations in Andalucía:

First Course: Caldo de puchero—chicken broth with potatoes, garbanzo beans, garden vegetables and tocino—salt pork. After it has simmered on the stove for a while the contents are strained to produce a rich hearty broth. Before serving, boiled rice, chopped hard- boiled egg and tiny pieces of jamón serrano are added.

Second Course: Pollo o pavo (chicken or turkey) accompanied by an ensalada or vegetables. Isabela confided that in the old days when life was hard and food was scarce, it was a feast to have chicken. In modern times of prosperity one might serve mariscos (shellfish: shrimp, lobsters) along with the typical tapa of manchego cheese and ibérico ham. Cordero al horno (roast lamb) or besugo al horno (baked sea bream) have been added to the list of foods.

Isabela listed the sweet treats for the Christmas season, many of which had Middle Eastern roots—they were globalized before it was fashionable! You can read more about some of these sweets in "Christmas Confections and Suffering Quince."
- Pestiños (honey-coated sweet fritters)
- Rosquitos (almond, honey, anisette, sugar)
- Rosco de navidad (cake, with inner fillings of chocolate, cream or sweetened pumpkin and syrup)
- Mazapán (marzipan)
- Turrón (honey and almonds with egg yolks, nuts, fruit, chocolate candy)
- Mantecados, polvorones (shortcake sweets made of shortening, honey and pulverized almonds), alfajores (orange-flavored shortbread which originated in Sevilla)
- Peladillas (almonds covered in white hard candy)

• Buñuelos (fried small portions of water, flour, anise seed and anisette dough—a little like donut holes)

Manzanilla, fino, and amontillado sherries are the most typical beverages, along with cava sparkling wine and anisette.

At midnight, the Christmas Eve gaiety is interrupted by ringing church bells, calling the families to "la Misa del Gallo." It is called the "Mass of the Rooster" because tradition says that the only time a rooster has ever crowed at midnight was on the day that Jesus was born.

Another long-standing tradition is to visit the "belén" or nativity scene. Isabela recalled that some years ago individuals took great pride in the meticulous construction of the belén. Public and private entities—such as banks, neighborhood associations, flamenco associations and schools—would set up within their facilities their own belén and would hang a sign at the street entrance welcoming the general public to visit them.

Today the essential message of the manger in Bethlehem has become secularized. To construct a crèche is mainly a hobby, rather than an act of devotion. Every year people make their own nativity scenes and enter them in a contest. The local "Asociación de Belenistas" gathers a large number of small nativity scenes and exhibits them in a large show room run by city hall.

Isabela and her daughter Olga wanted to highlight one of the "must-see" Christmas season activities for children who live in Jerez de la Frontera. It is a visit to the Servant of their Majesties where they send "wish letters" for the Día de los Reyes Magos (Three Kings Day). The activity takes place in the local Moorish castle (!) and is sponsored by the Ayuntamiento (city government) of Jerez de la Frontera.

Approximately fifteen "servants" are there, dressed in Moorish clothes to greet the boys and girls and other members of their extended families. They entertain the children with games and stories while the boys and girls wait to talk to the "Mayordomo" (Paje Real).

Other servants have desks where they issue and stamp certificates for the submission of the children's wish letters. The setting is amazing, very realistic for the children and exciting for all! It gets better every year!

Celebrating a Christian holiday in a Moorish Castle! I wish these two cultures could get along that well in the "real" world. Perhaps it is something to pray for.

Christmas in Andalucía, a Reflection: Miguel Valdespino

Traditional Spaniards view their extended family—all the uncles and aunts and cousins—as their lifeblood, their identity. But it goes beyond this; their neighborhood is included as part of their family in a broader sense, regardless of social position.

This neighborly bond is renewed daily in the custom of regularly stopping by a local tapas bar café to visit with friends. It is further reinforced when everyone, rich and poor alike, participates in the many fiestas that punctuate each year. The most dominant is the celebration of Navidad or Christmas, which extends from Advent through Three Kings Day—almost a whole month set aside for family renewal and social bonding!

In 2007 I asked my dear friend Isabela about her memory of Christmas in the sherry town of Jerez de la Frontera. You can read about it in "Christmas in Jerez de la Frontera."

In 2008 I asked another good friend, Miguel Valdespino, to recall his experience of Christmas. He is from an old family that arrived in Jerez de la Frontera in 1264, when it was still a frontier. Jerez was reconquered by one of Miguel's kin. You can read more about his family in "Valdespino: 700 Years of Family History." The Valdespinos have quite a different background from the Díaz family. Nevertheless they share a generous and intimate view of life, which is the essence of the Spanish spirit. The friendship that Miguel has extended to me has been remarkable. I think you will pick up a sense of his warmth and that of his family as you read the note he sent me.

Dear Don,

These are memories as they come, as if we were sitting at the plaza in Sanlúcar, having a glass of manzanilla and, as you say, tortillitas de camarones, and are therefore totally spontaneous.

In my younger days, up to my early teens, Christmas and New Year's Eve were spent in our home in Jerez de la Frontera. The great event was Christmas Eve, which we call La Nochebuena or the Good Night. Midnight Mass was popularly called Misa del Gallo, Mass of the Rooster because the long and elaborate celebration of the Eucharist almost stretched to dawn—about the time when the cocks crowed. Then we would have dinner and carols as we gathered around the Belén (manger scene or crèche).

Since 1990, when my mother-in-law died, we have celebrated La Nochebuena with my wife's side of the family as we gather for dinner. We are happy to be in the spacious house of Carmen, which is very close to our mutual parish church. She has eight very willing children that help with dinner, build a wonderful Belén, and both individually and as a chorus sing the most touching of religious carols.

The Belén is formed on a big table. It depicts the birth of Jesús: along with the Three Kings and a number of shepherds, sheep, donkeys, green-dyed sawdust and the inevitable "river" made of the "silver paper" that covered chocolate blocks.

"Midnight" Mass now begins at 9:00 PM. All members of our family attend the whole ceremony together, from infants a few months old to the older members. Last year we were sixty-three people at Mass. At the church after Mass there is the ceremony of kissing the foot of Baby Jesús who is lying in the manger. We then wish our dear priest Happy Christmas and the whole family walks across the street for dinner, at about 11:00 PM.

Each part of the family provides some special dishes as well as some small presents that a Papa Noel gives especially to children but also to grown-ups. The first course of the Nochebuena dinner is a cold buffet, accompanied by cups of hot consommé and various one-bite hot tapas. Included are tiny jamón Ibérico sandwiches and all sort of imaginative snacks. The ladies meet ahead of time for a three to four hour long "merienda"—afternoon tea—of which fifteen minutes is dedicated to discussing the menu.

Everything has to be homemade, except of course for the "turrón" and other classics like "polvorones" and "alfajores," reminiscent of

Arab culture. Boneless, stuffed, cold turkey is a must. This is followed by all types of shrimp salads, many of them made of chilled diced potatoes boiled in the same water used to cook fresh gambas or langostinos, and mixed with extra virgin olive oil mayonnaise to make an "ensaladilla."

As for my part, it does not change. I make the jamón sandwiches, as I have the knack of cutting the slices of squares of bread diagonally. I make them very thin, filling them with a mix of minced Ibérico jamón and a little butter before they are cut into small classic triangles.

Traditionally, I also cook one of the main courses, which consists of a roast pork infused with brandy, oloroso and Pedro Ximénez wines, and aged PX vinegar. We also supply the family gathering with fino and a manzanilla "en rama" i.e. just lightly filtered, not treated for bottling. It has a delicious aroma but does not keep long.

On Christmas Eve, we give the children some small presents for them to play with during the holidays. The more important presents are still reserved for The Three Kings on 6 January; The whole event ends at about 5:00 AM on Christmas morning with only the very young having gone to sleep in an improvised nursery.

There are of course very moving moments as we briefly pray for all of our family who have died and, especially, for my daughter Mónica who died in a car accident at twenty years old. We remember the many happy summers at Villa Carmen she spent with all her cousins.

The host always ends by saying "never again" with her children winking behind her, meaning "until next year."

It has given me great pleasure to remember all this, but when I see the bundle of words on my computer I feel that you do not deserve the penalty of having to go through it but, it is you that asked.

Warm regards,
Miguel

I hope you enjoyed Miguel's reminiscences. Of course, in America we cannot replicate the continuity of families such as those of Miguel and María, whose roots are deep, and who have lived hundreds of years in the same location. Nevertheless, I think as a nation we realize the importance of renewing family. May you be able to experience the joy of breaking bread together at a family table.

Nochebuena in the Alpujarras Mountains

In 1997, Ruth and I booked plane tickets for the whole family to celebrate Christmas in a remote part of Spain. We drove directly to Granada, spent the night, and then headed southeast toward the area surrounding the mountain village of Cádiar, deep in the Alpujarra region. It is a unique area, a natural link between the Mediterranean coast and Sierra Nevada, towered over by Spain's highest peaks. It is there that the remnants of the Moors sequestered themselves after the fall of Granada in 1492 and the Ottoman troops landed soon thereafter. It is not far from the dramatic mountain town of Trevélez, where the local people cure a fabulous jamón serrano in the shadow of the highest mountain pass in Spain.

It was quite a different feeling than the commercial atmosphere of modern times. It seems that each year I resolve to celebrate the Christmas season as people did in much simpler times. In 2010 these musings were prompted when I heard the notes of "Little Drummer Boy" wafting over the Musak system at Wal-Mart while people were sorting through Halloween costumes for their children! Later I saw an advertising insert for a "Pre-Day-After-Thanksgiving Day Sale" tucked into our local newspaper.

Our trip was not under the most auspicious of circumstances—spontaneous decisions seldom are. 1997 turned out to be the year when much of Spain was experiencing drenching rains and dramatic mudslides of historic proportions. Undaunted by the rain, we navigated the narrow mountain roads in two cars—each driver experiencing his own challenges as we snaked up the mountain range. The least of our worries were the few remaining roadside guardrails, which had been violently uprooted by the mud.

The road leading to the inn had been washed out by a mudslide. We stopped to ask directions from a man alongside the road. He hopped on our hood and guided us down the road. As one of our cars approached its destination, a horse started galloping behind us!

It was dark by the time we reached the end of our journey. But for the brilliant full moon and our guide, our destination would have been difficult to spot. Quite an adventure, but with a happy conclusion: the innkeeper greeted us and, with typical Spanish cordiality served us a simple and wholesome meal.

After a good night's sleep, we awakened to a sunny day in the clear mountain air. We were enjoying a respite from the stormy weather by climbing around on the rocks when our host asked us if we would like him to prepare for us a meal to celebrate La Nochebuena, Christmas Eve, which would be that evening. He noted that because of the weather there were few alternatives for us, and that he and his staff would be delighted to serve us. We gratefully accepted his kind offer.

The seven of us made our way to the village of Cádiar, stopping for some

The Harris family enjoys a Christmas Eve feast in the bodega of Alquería de Morayna, Cádiar (Granada)

café con leche and churros before arriving at a little shop in town to pick out amusing token gifts for each other. We decided to simplify gift giving by drawing names: each person would buy only one gift, and that gift could not exceed 500 pesetas ($3.00). As we drove back to our settlement we noticed the village parish church—a late medieval structure, perfect for Midnight Mass.

We returned to one of the most memorable meals we have ever shared together as a family. Our host had set up a long refectory-type table in his cellar bodega. We were surrounded by barrels of wine, and overhead dozens of serrano hams hung from the rafters. The wonderful aromas of the wine-soaked oak barrels and the still-curing jamones were soon augmented by the sweet smell of platters filled with roast legs of lamb—it seemed as if there was one for each one of us. The candle-lit table was laden with local vegetables and delicacies, accompanied by wine of the region. The feast continued on with Christmas sweets and savories, reaching its conclusion with glasses of brandy. No honey-coated spiral ham for us! We felt we were far away from modern America.

After dinner, as we were opening our little gifts we noticed the wind gusting stronger, until finally we lost electricity. But that did not stop us from getting ready to go to the ancient church in the village. As we were driving to town, our way illumined by the full moon, I romanticized how the lack of electricity would enhance our worship with the people of the village. It would be easy to imagine ourselves living in simpler times, centuries in the past.

We arrived at the church only a minute or two before midnight, relieved that we were not too late. But to our dismay we found a darkened church with the door locked! Just about then the local parish priest roared up in his small SEAT 600 sedan (so much for medieval illusions!). He greeted us, unlocked the door, and then bustled about the building, lighting several portable butane heaters and rolling them to where the congregation would be sitting. He saved one heater for himself by the altar.

Without electricity the medieval church did have an added charm—the flickering candles, the shadowy arches, the crèche in the transept, the villagers filtering in throughout the liturgy at their own pace. By the time Mass was over and the villagers were filing by the manger scene venerating the Christ child, the church was comfortably full.

What a blessed day it had been: our family together; the feast prepared by our innkeeper and served by young women from the town; opening modest presents and then worshiping together. It had been all that I could hope for—mudslides and lost electricity notwithstanding.

I know we cannot replicate this. The logistics are more complicated: our family has grown larger, two more sons are married; there are four grandchildren. But the commitment to greater simplicity during the holidays can be accomplished, and you do not have to go to Spain to do it. We discovered this truth a few years later here in Williamsburg, Virginia. We had a horrendous ice storm during the holidays, which knocked out our electricity and water for days. On Christmas Eve we tossed on a couple more logs, and sang carols by the crackling fire. It was that simple.

For many people Christmas is the favorite holiday of the year. No matter what our personal faith, the universal icon of mother and newborn child reflects hope, and the joy of loving families. This is the season for each of us to renew personal ties and extend ourselves to others, so that the shortest days of the year are filled with light and joy.

Noche Vieja:
Remembering the Year Past

A few years ago, we discovered that the Spanish celebration of what we think of as New Year's Eve provides another affirmation of the importance of family in that culture. Ruth and I were standing in a central plaza in the city of Córdoba with our three little boys on the last night of the year. As the hands of the clock progressed toward midnight, we expected to be engulfed by merry-makers eagerly anticipating the advent of the New Year.

If we were in America we would have felt from the crowd an air of expectant optimism that is typical of the American spirit: out with the old, in with the new. The new year will always be better, and will bring new opportunities for those ready to claim them. In Córdoba the atmosphere was quite different.

As the clock struck midnight, people were only beginning to assemble in the plaza. I wondered, "Where is everyone?" Then I chuckled to myself, thinking, "I should have remembered that the people of Andalucía are hardly ever 'on time.'" But the sparse gathering at the stroke of midnight had nothing to do with wristwatches! Traditional Spaniards choose to be home with their families on New Year's Eve, rather than in the streets with strangers.

Continuity of life within the family is highly prized in Spain. For this reason, acknowledging the passing year is integral to welcoming the new. During the first part of the evening the family is apt to reminisce about the past year's events—you might name that Old Year's Eve—Noche Vieja.

Then, as midnight approaches, the family welcomes the New Year—Año Nuevo—with a glass of sparkling cava—often eating individual grapes—one for each toll from the bell tower. It is after people recall the

contributions of the past year that they go into the streets to celebrate
the coming year with neighbors. This way of marking the change of years
makes much more sense to me.

In much the same spirit as the Spaniards do when their families gather for
Noche Vieja, for the past forty-five years Ruth and I have vowed to write a
Christmas letter. I am sure some of you do the same thing. The letter recalls
personal events of the past year and reflects on what this means to us.

Our intent is good, but the execution is quite another. Our lives are so
busy that pausing to write the message becomes a burden; after many delays
it is often mailed out late, or not at all. This is a far cry from the true spirit of
Noche Vieja, swapping stories with family and friends at the dinner table!

This is yet another instance of allowing our quality of life to be compro-
mised when we assent to the demands of the fast-paced life. There is no
requirement that we conform to the artifices of our culture. We can intention-
ally set aside a quiet, intimate time of sharing with those we love. The traditional Spanish family does that as a matter of custom as they mark the end of
another year. We can enhance our lives by following their example.

The Joy of Children: Three Kings Day

Three Kings Day, on the sixth of January, is still alive and well in Spain. The local parades, the Magi, the happy children scrambling for caramelos—it is Epiphany, the culmination of Christmas festivities, and it remains intact—very traditional and very Spanish.

It is one of the religious celebrations that are central to Spain's identity. That most Spanish of all events, Semana Santa, is still so laden with emotion that the suffering of Good Friday almost eclipses the Resurrection as a focus of devotion and celebration.

Three Kings Day is quite different. Rather than being devotional, it is the festival for children and family. The celebration of the Wise Men's arrival is an official excuse to go all out, showering attention and affection on children, who are singularly treasured in Spanish culture.

Modern Spain has been heavily influenced by the modern secularism imported from America and her northern European neighbors. Santa, as a mercantile symbol, is in most stores. Modern Spaniards even have Christmas trees!

But if you want to experience traditional Spain, go to the towns and celebrate el Día de Reyes with the local people, where Three Kings Day is still central in children's hearts. The Christmas season begins with a Carta de Reyes, a letter that children pick up in the post office, fill out, and mail free of charge to the Three Wise Men.

On the eve of Epiphany, or Día de Reyes Magos, the three kings process down the main streets of Spain's towns. One of them, Baltasar, is an anachronism in that he appears as a Moor and an African, reflecting the long Muslim presence in Spain! He is a favorite of the children since, until recently, black

Africans were rarely seen in Spain. Baltasar is accompanied by the other Magi, Melchor and Gaspar. They toss candy into the excited crowd of children. In some towns, the Magi stop to greet the children personally, giving them small presents as well.

After the excitement of the parade, it is time to get the children ready for bed. Just before bedtime on this magic eve, the children prepare three items to leave by the door for the Wise Men: a dish of water and hay or straw for their camels, rich turrón made of honey and almonds, and a glass of wine or sherry for the kings. Next to these provisions the children leave a pair of shoes in which they hope the kings will deposit a gift or two.

When they awaken the next morning the children discover their gifts. For breakfast they might enjoy chocolate a la taza (thick hot chocolate) and roscón de reyes—sweet bread embedded with candied fruit. It is similar to Easter bread in Greece and Scandinavia. Within the bread is hidden a prize— perhaps a small coin or a ring. Whoever finds it is King or Queen for the Day.

Late in the afternoon, after dinner and a siesta, the children and their parents visit the homes of their extended family—grandparents, aunts and uncles, a favorite cousin—to see what the kings have given them. It is an all-day celebration devoted to family.

Ruth and I, and our sons, have many fond memories of Día de Reyes. One year we visited Guadalupe. The village surrounding the Monastery of Guadalupe is nestled deep in the mountains of the same name. The town was a particular favorite of Ferdinand and Isabela. In fact, it was there that they received Columbus when he returned from his first voyage, bringing many exotic new foods such as peppers, tomatoes and chocolate.

The year that we visited Guadalupe the weather was a little raw; wind and mist were blowing in from the mountains. However the weather did not dampen the spirit of the townspeople. From the steps under the fourteenth-century Mudéjar facade of the monastery, the mayor read the names of children who had been born into their community during the previous year. As each child's name was announced, the parents brought their baby forward and up the steps, where the infant was blessed by the priest and given a little gift from the town.

Then from the distance we heard the rhythm of drums that local young men were beating, heralding the arrival of the Three Kings. Down a side street they came, on flatbeds pulled by John Deere tractors. They slowly wended their way into the plaza mayor. For us adult literalists, a tractor has little resemblance to a camel or a horse, but that did not faze the delighted children as they scrambled for the candy, which was liberally sown.

Our favorite Día de Reyes celebration took place in the jewel of a village named Trujillo, in Extremadura, western Spain. It has been such a quiet town for so long that the Pizarro brothers left for the New World hundreds of years ago in search of excitement and adventure. The entire population gathers in the vast Plaza Mayor the evening before Día de Reyes, under the watchful eye of Conquistador Juan Pizarro, who is looking down from a huge bronze statue.

As we stood among the gathering we could see grandmothers lovingly fussing over grandchildren safely tucked in their strollers. Fathers and grand-fathers were playing with the young boys, who were scampering through the crowd of their neighbors.

Families would stop to admire the belén, or crèche, situated in the plaza near the stone steps. A beautiful young girl next to the manger was dressed as Mary. She was watched over by a young boy, Joseph, who was a little less convincing with his cotton-batting beard. Gathered around the manger were a handful of teen-aged shepherds.

A clatter of hoofs echoing off the cobblestones indicated the pending arrival of the Three Kings—three young fathers riding horses from their farms. The whole village had gathered in the plaza to greet them: young parents with babes in arms, grandmothers peering proudly into baby carriages delivering a couple of caramelos (hard candies) to their delighted grand-children, and lots of excited kids circling about the plaza. Eventually they migrated to the side street where the Three Kings had settled to greet the children personally and give them presents.

Perhaps the most elaborate festivity we witnessed was in the holy city of Santiago de Compostela—the goal for pilgrims throughout the world. It was dusk as we walked in the mist across the Plaza del Obradoiro. From the direction of the cathedral on our left, shrouded with fog, I could hear the haunting notes of a jazz saxophone played by a young pilgrim whose figure I could barely make out in the archway.

The ancient stone arcades of the pilgrimage town were alive with hundreds of excited children crowding the curbs to get a better look at the Magi. As we headed across the Plaza toward the cabalgata (cavalcade) of the Kings, we were jostled by the crowding of parents and grandparents who were making sure their little children did not miss out.

We peered around the medieval stone columns of Santiago's ancient Romanesque arcades to witness the arrival of the Magi. Their entrance was quite impressive—out of the misty night appeared three men in elaborate costumes, mounted on steeds and accompanied by truck after truck of caramelos for the children. There were more wrapped candies than I had ever seen in one place! So much life! So much joy! To think that children have been crowding these curbs for centuries!

What a wonderful way to end the holiday season—providing some event to delight our children. I mentioned earlier that Spaniards treasure their children, and I used the word "treasured" purposely. If there is one characteristic above all others that attracts me to Spain, it is seeing how the whole community loves their children.

Other mothers (and grandmothers), whom we would view as strangers, will joyfully come up to a little baby and admire her profusely. Then they will reach into their purse for a caramelo to present to the child. ¡Qué guapa!—How beautiful!—she will exclaim. Those women are not strangers but part of a broader community that supports the child all of her (or his) life.

The English adage "children should be seen and not heard" is incomprehensible to the traditional Spaniard. As many of you know who have traveled the byways of Spain, children are everywhere. When Ruth and I were eating dinner at 10:00 PM in Andalucía, we would see Spanish parents enjoying dinner together, while all around their tables the children were playing. And why not? They are as much part of the family as the older people. In fact they are our hope.

¡Hola!

7
Closing Thoughts

Salinero de Vicente Family: Salinero de Vicente, Garat Salinero, Ricbour Salinero and Cascajosa Salinero

The Heart of Spain

What is at the heart of Spain? It is being together as a family, and the special way in which they cherish their children. This begins with the experience of young childhood where the little boy or girl is showered with love within the family, and treasured by the neighborhood. There is no fear of "spoiling" the child.

The heart of Spain is fostered by daily encounters of affection expressed within the family and neighborhood. From a childhood immersed in seemingly unconditional love, comes an eagerness to engage in personal interchange, and a willingness to maintain these personal relationships through frequent contact. When one begins life with this kind of affirmation, it becomes second nature to engage friend and stranger alike with a kind personal intimacy.

The companionship of their family soon extends to all those whom they touch. Spaniards refer to people by their given name; in greeting they embrace even the stranger; they acknowledge fellow diners; they sit shoulder to shoulder in the bullring. It is an intimacy that comes from treating one another as sacred, as people of worth.

Needless to say, mine is an idealized image; we are all flawed human beings affected by the vicissitudes of life. That being said, it is this foundation of caring through the communal experience that endows Spaniards with a certain dignity and grace, and a willingness to engage the world with hospitality. Theirs is not a closed society where the value of privacy is elevated; it has always been a way of life that is warm and welcoming.

Uncles and aunts, cousins and grandparents are next-door neighbors. They see each other several times a week while shopping at the local market or at their favorite tapas bar. Members of the family often operate local shops, work together in the fields, or man the fishing boats. These kinds of relationships stand the test of time, and mature throughout the years of one's life. Even today, this is the customary way of life throughout much of Spain.

Their traditions find roots in a preindustrial society, where the natural cycles of the seasons, from planting to harvest, encouraged a stable way of life. Even though there have been some profound changes in the social structure of Spain during the past twenty or thirty years, the foundational values of integrated family loyalty and mutual support are still in place.

Just the other day I was reminded of the sense of family and community that is the heart of Spain when I attended a wine-tasting at our store in Williamsburg. We were featuring wines of an artisan sherry bodega, Gutiérrez-Colosía. When I initiated a conversation with the owners, Carmen and Juan Carlos, their immediate response to me was extraordinarily warm and welcoming.

Soon our son Jonathan and his wife Stacey joined the conversation and before we knew it, over a glass of wine Carmen started planning a party for our family at their bodega in Spain—complete with manzanilla and the freshest seafood from her friend Eugenio. She told me that she would include us as along with our son Tim and his family, who are currently living in El Puerto de Santa María, not far from their winery.

Mind you, this was not just an empty pleasantry. Two weeks later, she was true to her word. Ruth and I had hardly stepped off the airplane before our family was invited to join Juan Carlos and Carmen in their bodega to witness a flamenco performance. It was followed by an evening at the local feria (fair) where we enjoyed sherry with Carmen and Juan Carlos's lifelong friends.

In Carmen's society cousins, families, and friends continue to network seamlessly. A few days after meeting her at our store, I received an email from Carmen saying that since she was now back home in Spain, she was planning to contact her cousins to find a place for Stacey and her family since they were going to stay in El Puerto for several months next year! "It will be nice for us to have them as neighbors," she wrote, "We could play paddleball together."

The development of our society in America comes from a distinctly different base than that of traditional Spain with her continuity of generations. From its foundation, the United States has been formed by waves of people who have arrived from many different homelands and traditions. Because they were not bound by the expectations of an older culture, these new Americans were liberated from their past. However, their individual freedom was acquired at the cost of losing a sense of belonging.

As a result, the United States is a young and flexible country, but with fragile family roots. It is not uncommon in America for parents to live in one state and their children to live in another hundreds of miles away. I have friends who fly 4,000 miles from Richmond to Anchorage in order to see their grandchildren for a week or two every year!

This experience of family separation was brought home to me while I was attending our annual La Tienda party. Every year the Harris family hosts an evening with the La Tienda "family" where we thank them for their hard work during the holiday rush. The 2009 party was especially memorable because we were together in our new La Tienda retail store, an historic farmhouse and potter's studio that we have transformed to reflect the *ambiente* of Spain.

As I enjoyed tapas with our employees and their families, it occurred to me that we were a veritable United Nations! There were people from a dozen different countries: Portugal, Spain, Cuba, Bolivia, Dominican Republic, El Salvador, Greece, India, Brazil, the Philippines, Puerto Rico and, of course, the United States. Not that we had planned it that way: this is America!

Most of these industrious men and women have come to the United States to make a better life, just as my grandparents did around the turn of the twentieth century. However, there is a cost, often overlooked, that is integral to their decision to come to America: they are separated from generations of their families who remain behind.

We were with many proud parents whose happy children scampered from room to room. However, most of the families there are not able to replicate the traditional extended family structure that Ruth, I, and our children enjoy, and that I write about in my essays. They live far from parents, brothers, and sisters whom they hold dear. Their children do not grow up close to uncles and aunts, cousins and grandparents.

This is a significant loss. They need to find other ways to maintain family ties and make a healthy life for themselves and their children. However, necessity is the mother of invention, especially in America. What I learned in talking with our fellow workers is that some of them have been ingenious in maintaining close ties with those back home.

One example is Nirav from India. His father feels strongly that his family should eat together around a common table every day. Therefore, Nirav and his parents have a standing appointment once a week. Every Saturday morning Nirav gets up, takes a shower and dresses in a careful manner. Then he sets the table for breakfast in front of his computer. When all the elements are assembled, he "Skypes" his parents in India. Anticipating the call, Nirav's parents have set the table for their evening meal. When they are connected via Skype, Nirav and his parents share conversation and a common meal, or at least a common mealtime via video.

Nirav has taken advantage of this remarkable new technology to be with his family on the other side of the world. He told me wryly that he spends more time with his parents now than when he lived in India with the myriad distractions that are part of a young man's fast-paced life. He has compensated for the realities of twenty-first century life in which traditional bonds are strained by geography.

What I am describing in both the Spanish sherry families and the new Americans is what is fashionably described as "social networking." I see Twitter, Facebook, Skype, You Tube and even ancestry.com ("the world's largest on line resource for family history"), as modern attempts to address the downside of personal autonomy with its frayed family connections. It is an electronic attempt to reconnect and to rebuild the bridges that were always in place in the earlier society and still remain in much of Spain.

Magical as it may seem, an Internet connection is no more than a dispassionate tool to accomplish an end that you determine as the user. If you have a sense of engagement and responsibility toward people around you, then these new means now available are immeasurably positive. The opportunity for visual connection with loved ones wherever they may be, is extraordinary.

However, in an individualistic society that prizes autonomy over interdependence, it can do harm to your soul, through the way you treat others in our common journey through life. Facebook requires you to sort out impersonally whom you want to designate as "friends" and to discard the others without their knowledge. By employing an impersonal technique, the "Caller ID" feature on your phone enables you to determine whether you want to talk to a person, or to ignore him—it helps you cull out the unwanted, or the inconvenient person while avoiding any personal contact with them.

As with every modern advance, technology can be a tool to enrich one's life, or to insulate us further in an impersonal world where simulated voices "chat" with you when you call for a service to be performed. This is why it is so important that we fill our hearts with human contacts, as our Spanish neighbors do.

There is nothing that can assure our spiritual well being more than a loving, caring human presence. We can never replace the experience of hospitality conveyed face to face—and why should we? It is this *duende*—a difficult to define Spanish phrase that connotes emotion and authenticity—that is the heart of Spain. It is also her gift to the world.

ACKNOWLEDGMENTS

Tina Cores and Zaida Rivera, who selflessly helped our family launch La Tienda in the early days, when we hung jamones in our basement, and stored olives in the garage.

Pilar Vico, a mainstay of the Spanish National Tourist Office, New York—a warm and caring professional, and a treasured friend who has provided me years of friendly counsel—drawing upon her deep knowledge of her native land.

Penélope Casas, a gifted writer and dear friend, who was on the vanguard of Spanish cooking. With Luís her loving husband and lifetime companion, she contributed so much support and guidance as Ruth and I discovered Spain.

Cynthia Joba, my bright and engaging editor and amiga, whose ability to bring a sense of order from my many years of writings was extraordinary, as were her patience, integrity and wit.

Patricia Searl who faithfully worked at my side in Williamsburg. She helped me select from the countless pictures of Spain, and gently helped me tame the gremlins of computer composition.

Olga Díaz Buzón, whom I have known since she was a little girl. For many years, she has faithfully translated my monthly Reflections into Spanish for LaTienda.com. Her assistance in proof reading this manuscript with a Spanish eye has been invaluable.

And I must not forget loyal Hayk, my Armenian Street Dog with a heart of gold. As I labored over this manuscript, he was my constant companion, peacefully lying next to me on a rug from his native land.

PHOTO CREDITS

p. x, Jim Fernandez—Jim Fernandez

p. xvi, Society of Spain Awards—Society of Spain

p. xxviii, Some people thought he was a saint—
©Ergor85 | Dreamstime.com

p. 17, Castrillo de los Polvazares—©Scott Martin

p. 21, Handmade, award-winning manchego—La
Tienda

p. 23, Membrillo—La Tienda

p. 31, Pigs and dehesa—Sánchez Romero Carvajál

p. 33, Happy pig—Sánchez Romero Carvajál

p. 47, Minaya, long ago—Princesa de Minaya

p. 49, Lola León Gallego—Envasados Lola S.A.

p. 49, Lola León Gallego, Amalia Moreno Conejo,
Margarita Almagro Calderón, Paqui Hermoso
Palomino, Ana Sierra Rosales—Envasados
Lola S.A.

p. 57, A feast!—La Tienda

p. 58, Paella party—La Tienda

p. 60, José and Amalia Salcedo—El Navarrico S.A.

p. 89, Croquetas de Bacalao—La Tienda

p. 94, El Puente del Arzobispo—©Arno
Klinkhamer | andaluciaimagen.com

p. 96, Augustín de la Cal Berreira, Maestro
Artesano—Belén de la Cal Hidalgo

p. 96, Painter Belén de la Cal Hidalgo, daughter—
Belén de la Cal Hidalgo

p. 100, Cazuelas—La Tienda

p. 121, Pedro Díaz—Olga Díaz Buzón

p. 122, Pedro the sailor at U.S. Naval Hospital—
unknown, supplied by Olga Díaz Buzón

p. 123, Pedro Díaz and his wife Isabela as
newlyweds—unknown, supplied by Olga Díaz
Buzón

p. 123, Pedro Díaz and his wife Isabella—Olga
Díaz Buzón

p. 132, Treaty of Tordesillas—Archivo General de
Indias (Spain)—public domain

p. 145, Arco de la Pastora, Medina Sidonia—
©José Luis Trullo| | andaluciaimagen.com

p. 150, King Juan Carlos talks with his son Prince
Felipe—©Javier Soriano/AFP/Getty Images

p. 153, Rafael Nadal, Rogers Cup 2008
(Toronto)—©Zairbek Mansurov | dreamstime.
com

p. 157, Tomás Lozano—Tomás Lozano

p. 158, Tomás playing with his father—Lozano
family

p. 158, Tomás with his father and cousin Carmen
—Lozano family

p. 177, Tomb of the Lovers of Teruel—Wikimedia
Commons user Montrealais (cc-by-sa-2.5)

p. 181, El Albaicín on a spring night, Granada—
©Jesús Puertas | andaluciaimagen.com

p. 186, Falla Statue, Fallas de Valencia—©Lola |
Dreamstime.com

p. 191, Plaza Mayor, El Rocío (Huelva)—
©Laurent | andaluciaimagen.com

p. 211, "Monaguillo tocando la zambomba";
Ignacio Pinazo Camarlench; Oil on canvas;
1893–95—Museo de Bellas Artes de Valencia

p. 225, Three Kings parading in Sevilla—©Valeria
Cantone | dreamstime.com

p. 230, Flock of sheep—©Daniel Acevedo |
andaluciaimagen.com

p. 232, Salinero de Vicente Family: Salinero de
Vicente, Garat Salinero, Ricbour Salinero
and Cascajosa Salinero—Patricia Salinero de
Vicente

All photographs not credited on this page were
taken by members of the Harris family.